WHEN
SUMMER'S
IN
THE
MEADOW

WHEN SUMMER'S IN THE MEADOW

Niall Williams
and
Christine Breen

SOHO

Copyright © 1989 by Niall Williams and Christine Breen.
All rights reserved under International and Pan-American
Copyright Conventions
Published in the United States of American by Soho Press, Inc.
1 Union Square
New York, N.Y. 10003

Library of Congress Cataloging-in-Publication Data

Williams, Niall, 1958–
    When summer's in the meadow / by Niall Williams and
    Christine Breen.
        p.   cm.
      ISBN 0-939149-23-0
        1. Ireland—Biography. 2. Williams, Niall, 1958–   3. Breen,
Christine, 1954–   4. Farm life—Ireland—History-20th century.
5. Ireland—Social life and customs—20th century. I. Breen,
Christine, 1954–   II. Title.
CT866.W54 1989
941.9'3—dc19
[B]   88-30265
CIP

Manufactured in the United States of America

First Edition
First Printing

DEDICATION

This book is dedicated to our families,
to our friends in Ireland and America,
but most of all
to Deirdre.

AUTHORS' NOTE

Once again, this book was written by two people. No episode belonged exclusively to either of us—whether in the living or the writing. Sections were drawn from both our journals and both of our pens have had a part in every page.

WHEN
SUMMER'S
IN
THE
MEADOW

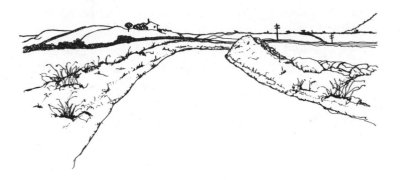

CHAPTER ONE

It was raining softly. I was standing at the gate to the back meadow in the early morning, gazing up across the hill fields of Tumper. Nothing was moving. No sound came or went on the Kiltumper road. A pale gray sky seemed to sit down, drizzling, over the day. I was looking up at our little herd of four cows and thinking of the winter just ahead. There was a fine stack of turf in the haybarn, and a low mound of silage, fodder for the cattle. They were on their last grazing on the hills, and would soon have to be brought down closer to the cottage. That morning in the light rain I looked up at them and wondered a little at the life Chris and I were living in west Clare. It had already been a year and a half since we moved here from New York, and now the tremendous silence of these wet November days was shaped by each morning's writing in the parlor and the watching, feeding, and herding of Susie, Phoebe, Bridget, and Gerty, our cows.

As I stood by the dripping ash trees in the back haggard, where the haybarn is, I thought I saw something small and black moving in the upper field. Too small to be a calf, too large for a dog, it darted back and forth by the far wall, causing the cows to scatter. At once I headed out across the fields, brushing a dark trail through the silvery rain drops beading the grass. I crossed the stone walls with a little urgency in my stride. Here, as if to order, was an indication of how different our lives had become since leaving our careers in New York. Marching up the fields in the rain with a blackthorn stick in my hand was now my main business. The first item on this morning's agenda was to attend to our unsettled cows.

Halfway up Lower Tumper I saw it clearly: a shaggy black goat with long horns, chomping on the prickly green leaves of a gorse bush.

"Get up, go on, out of it! Go on!" I shouted, raising my stick and thrashing the air.

Lifting its head a moment to gaze at me, the goat bleated twice and went back to its breakfast. There was a chewed end of old rope still tied around its hind leg, and it was obvious that it had escaped that morning from some farm in the neighborhood.

"Come on," I yelled again, trying hard to sound as if I meant it. "Back where you came from, go on!"

This time, as I closed in on it, the goat moved with some speed and agility, scampering away ahead of me and making the poor jittery cows charge off down the field in a panic. Here it must be said in my defence, I had absolutely no experience of goats, and that morning I decided that the quickest solution to the problem was to handle the goat like any other stray animal, driving it first from the field

2

out onto the road, then down into one of the stone cabins (sheds) below, where I would lock it in until the owner was found. It all seemed perfectly reasonable and straightforward, if a little urgent now that the rain was steadily sweeping in over us from the west. So, with a number of very serious yells, waving my stick masterfully in front of me, I began to drive the goat down the beaten grass track to the gate below. Every second yell or so, the goat trotted on a little ahead of me, bleating and turning a mistrustful eye back to where my stick, like a sword, pointed the way.

The gate, of course, was tied shut. Ten yards or so before we reached it, I ran around in front of my prisoner and untied the cord, letting the gate swing open onto the road. With its head on one side, the goat watched me and slowly chewed over the grass in its mouth. Making a wide half-circle, I hurried up and around behind it, once more giving a few sharp yells and brandishing the blackthorn. On we went, little by little, the goat a few steps ahead of me and the gate coming nearer at every moment. As we reached it, I moved in closer to the animal.

"Go on! Go on, get out there! Go on."

With a sudden little trot the goat was out of the field, onto the verge of the road and away from our cows. Leaving it standing there a second, I turned to retie the cord on the gate. Even as I was doing it, congratulating myself on my handling of the little farm maneuver and thinking of going home to dry off before the fire, I heard the swift clattering of the goat's footsteps on the gravel, and turning, was just in time to see the flash of horns and hair as the goat ran up alongside the gate, and effortlessly jumped over the wall and back into the field. It looked at me through the locked gate for a moment, bleated at the stupidity of the whole exercise, and then went happily running off up the field to breakfast on the gorse once more and unnerve our cows in the process.

Drying off by the turf-fire in the kitchen, I described the situation to Chris.

"Well, we have to find out who it belongs to," she said. "They're probably looking for it. Call Gregory and tell him."

Gregory was the postmaster and telephone operator in the village. We no longer twirled the little crank handle on the upside-down telephone that still hangs on our wall. Progress in telephone communication had reached us in Kiltumper. Now we could tap into a source of community information by ringing him directly ourselves. The post office, like the church, was a kind of central intelligence; Gregory would know if a goat was gone missing or he would find out simply by asking his customers—nearly the entire village.

"Hello, Gregory?"

"Yes."

"Gregory, did you hear of anyone losing a goat up around us?"

"A goat?" He paused, the line crackled. "What kind of goat is it?" he asked, reasonably enough.

I had no idea. Breed, sex, even accurate size had been lost on me. I didn't yet know enough about goats to make these fine distinctions.

"A black goat," I said. "I found it in among our cows this morning."

"No," he said, "I haven't heard of anyone losing one. But it's with your cows is it?"

"Yes."

"Well, I'll ask around for you, okay?" he offered helpfully.

That evening we took the question out on the *cuaird*—when we went visiting. We walked down the road to of our good neighbor Mary's cozy kitchen. There we sat down to a welcome of tea and buns and spoke over the spattering of the nighttime rain blowing invisibly against the windows.

"We have a goat, Mary," said Chris.

"Have ye? A goat, Crissie, that's lovely. What are you going to do with him? Or is it a her?"

"That's just it," said Chris, amused at my inability to provide this information with certainty.

"It isn't ours, Mary," I said. "It was up among the cows this morning and it's there still. There's a bit of rope tied to one its legs so it must have escaped from somebody. I'm sure they're looking for it."

We sipped our tea and listened to the dark rain outside.

"Maybe, Niall," said Mary. "Is it an old goat?"

Again, I didn't really know, but I had seen gray in the goat's beard and said it was, even as I wondered if female goats had in fact got beards at all.

"Well, I like the goat," said Chris suddenly, "and it won't really harm the cows, will it, Mary?"

"Indeed she won't, Crissie. Once the cows get used to her they'll be fine. And do you know they say goats are very lucky with cows. She'll eat all the poisonous herbs and that. She could be very lucky with ye."

She could be very lucky with ye. That evening we didn't think much more about what Mary had said. Only as we looked back later did it seem that so much had have begun that day with the arrival of the goat in Kiltumper.

She was a bearded-lady goat as it turned out. No one in the village claimed her. Within a week the cows had grown used to her. And the look she gave me as I walked up the hill fields with the blackthorn stick seemed to say: Don't drive me away, I could be lucky for ye yet.

How was it all going, then?

We had been here since the end of March 1985, eighteen of the wettest, funniest, happiest, saddest, most extraordinary months of our lives. Now, we were spending our second winter in our little cottage in Kiltumper. Letters arrived, from time to time, were deposited in the

5

biscuit-tin letterbox at the foot of the path by our postman, P. J. Crowley, and opened by us. And each of them asked the same question: *How is it all going?* Had we had enough? For by now, surely, the last romantic gleam of our rural retreat must have vanished? We had suffered through two of the wettest summers in recent Irish history, cold, damp springs, and a colder, damper winter in a cottage heated only by a turf fire. Surely we were ready to come back now? "Manhattan is waiting," the letters seemed to say, "all is forgiven."

No, we were not ready to go back. For here in the rains of Kiltumper, in the very house where Chris's grandfather had been born, we had *found* something that we had come in search of. As Chris had written in her journal: "We have found the framework for a peaceful life. And despite the loneliness that sometimes seems invasive and the pain of childlessness, we have chosen to remain committed to our new way of life."

In the wind and the rain of west Clare we had become part of a community, made new friends like Lucy and Larry, Tessie and Jay, Martin and Martin (among a whole host of extraordinarily welcoming and generous neighbors); we had learned the rhythms of land, the ways of west Clare farming, and a sundry of daily things that were integral to the life about us. We had discovered a new way of living. We had Bridget, Susie, Phoebe, and Gerty; we had our hens and chickens, and Max, our black cat. With them, we had formed a unit here within which there was a very real and tangible sense of peace. Caring for them, tending and nursing the flower and vegetable gardens through all seasons, we had been able to put aside some of our grief when a trip to Dublin had confirmed that we were unable to have children. The garden, the farm, and our neighbors had come to mean so much to us. In the hush, on twilight evenings, walking back along the western road toward the sea, it sometimes seemed to both of us that the axis of our lives had shifted profoundly. No, we were not going back now was my response. Or, as Chris would say, not yet.

Poring over catalogs of seeds and bulbs, Chris spent these winter hours replanning the garden. There were more perennial daisies, phlox, and oriental poppies to go in, she told me, handing over the latest pen-and-ink drawing of the garden-to-be, and showing where the giant mound of ancestral rhubarb had, in a single pen stroke, been shifted from beneath the kitchen window, and the flower bed extended all the way across the front of the cottage.

In our dreams of next spring, we had tried to answer the question of the duration of our stay here. We had stored fodder for the cows and litter for bedding for their calves. We had plans to cut turf early in April and have the haybarn full by the following summer. But meanwhile, the last of our savings from New York had dwindled to near nothing. A three-hundred-page manuscript telling the adventure of our first year here had been sent in the post to America. As weeks passed and we waited for some response, our hopes of earning by our writing some of the money we would soon need in earnest began to seem ephemeral. But it was still a hope we clung to, like our hope of a fine spring. Suddenly, in a clutch of panic, we felt very isolated. We jumped into the old Peugeot and drove through the last daylight to watch the heady tumble of the sea, looking out towards the west.

"It's going to be lovely weather this year, Crissie," Mary promised, as we sat over tea mugs looking out at another winter day of spilling rain. "Do ye know, the year before ye came was a great year now, and the one before that, too. Everyone was brown as berries, and this summer'll be the same, now, for you," she said with a great smile as if, with that, the weather had been decided, and it was time for more tea. We trudged home through sheets of rain.

The spring and summer of 1987 were to be our salvation. They were to erase the memories of two years' puddled bog, the lakelike fields of lost hay, the drowned and ragged garden, the sense we couldn't quite shake that we had been dogged with bad luck here. No, the wet mud of last year's soil would be baked dry and fine *this* year, I assured Chris. I knew in my heart that the pain of our childlessness was more daunting than the failure of any other of our hopes. The constant rains seemed to drive us in upon ourselves, locking us in the little room of our grief. This spring and summer *would* come, I promised. The sun would be there in the mornings when we woke, and, going out early into the magnificent hush and stillness of the countryside all around us, we would potter through the brightness, tending to Chris's long-imagined garden as if working and reworking the very stuff of a dream. In the soft warmth of summertime we would sit upon the window ledge that looks down across the potato ridges and away, greenly southwards, to Kerry. In the afternoons and evenings there would be hay to save, ours and our neighbors, and then quiet hours in the cut meadows stippled with haystacks. We would feel the warm glow we sometimes longed for in midwinter when we tightened our coats, saw our breath fade on the air, and yearned for the coming of summer.

From the heart of midwinter Kiltumper we hoped that the spring and summer of 1987 would give us proof that we had not been completely foolish to have uprooted ourselves, to have journeyed from Manhattan to the west of Ireland, to have left the "real world" for the unearthly silence of the bogs and the rain. Everyone said our first two summers had been the worst in a hundred years. We needed a sign, a token that the future would be better.

I knew in my heart I couldn't expect Chris to continue living here in a climate without any sun. For myself, the problem was not really the weather. I am Irish, after all, and more used to the 'soft' weather we had been experiencing. It came and went outside the window of the quiet room where all morning I wrote; it drizzled and poured on the afternoons when I was out around the garden or up with the cows, but it never stopped my work or slowed my pen. No, for me, the fulfillment longed for by spring, or summer, was that the dreams and work of the past year and a half would at last bring in some money. We were all but bankrupt, and unless a publisher in New York bought the manuscript of our first year's adventures here, by mid summer we would be selling the cows, packing our suitcases, and giving up.

"But, Crissie," Mary said, "God is good, there'll never be another summer like them. . ."

Sipping our tea on a dull afternoon, we wanted, so desperately, to believe her.

Another thread of hope sustained us through the winter. Having been raised with four brothers and a dear sister, and having imagined from her very first days of playing house all her babies—the rooms they would have, the birthday parties, the little friends, the whole shape of things to come—Chris had been devastated by the prospect of childlessness. And so had I. Almost a year previously, we had picked up the telephone in the kitchen, twirled the knob, and made one of the most important calls of our lives: to St. Catherine's Adoption Society in Ennis. When a soft-spoken lady came on the line, she told us quite gently that the waiting list for adoption was closed. It might re-open again in April. But in April it was still closed. The number of couples seeking to adopt was still greater than the number of infants available. Try again in six months, we were told. Chris wrote in her journal:

Today, April 1, 1986, the waiting list to make an application for an adoption was supposed to be opened. Niall and I hoped at least to make a start in considering adoption as a way of having a family of our own. But it is still closed. I can't believe it. Helen, the social worker there, said they would reevaluate the situation again in October. What is going on? It seems that we are destined to remain childless. I cried when she told me. It seemed like another door was shut on me. During the last six months we've been learning to live with the idea of never having offspring of our own and wondering if adoption might not be the next best thing. Now we can't even explore that alternative. No babies.

Maybe we're just not ready. There is so much pain still and we've been torturing ourselves with it. We just have to let it go. We must try not to seek for the reason that God doesn't want us to be parents. Although now it seems true. Another six months of waiting. It doesn't seem fair to me.

On a bleak day in November, we sat in the car in O'Connell Street in the town of Ennis, again talking through the pain and loss we'd both felt since discovering we could not have children of our own. We watched women wheeling toddlers past us in the cold outside, the whole squealing, dribbling, giggling, bawling business of life itself flashing past the car window. We felt we had been cut off, set adrift in a kind of isolation by our prospect of childlessness. Life without children seemed even more empty in the great quiet of the cottage and countryside. We both felt a setting apart of those who were parents from childless couples. "But you've no children," said a woman in the village, nodding to herself, as if in that everything was explained, as if it was impossible for either of *us* to understand the daily trials and cares of parent-hood. Our grief, like a shadow, seemed always with us, unshakable, unlosable through a winter, spring, summer, and fall. We lived with it, some days more bearable than others, caring for the cat, the hens, the chickens, and the cows, as if they were part of our family.

Now we sat in the car outside St. Catherine's, not know-ing whether to go in and inquire about the waiting list, or not. Tears came so easily at the very moment we chided ourselves against self-pity. Were we meant to be childless then? Were we totally unsuited for parenthood? If, on this, our third time applying, we were still unable to get on the waiting list, then, perhaps, was it a sign that we must accept?

At last, we stepped from the car into the windy rain, and, feeling as if everyone in the world was watching us, walked down a narrow lane to St. Catherine's.

Clare Social Services, which encompasses St. Cather-ine's Adoption Society, has its offices in an old building which bears the telltale signs that it is an organization for helping and caring. It might once have been a primary school. Faint echoes of children in uniforms almost seem to resound through the long corridors and up the narrow staircases. Or perhaps it was once a convent, for there are also still sounds of prayer and peacefulness in the air. We found ourselves facing a tiny window closed by a wooden window door. To our surprise it suddenly opened. A gentle voice said, "May I help you?"

"Yes," I whispered, my voice faltering. "We'd like to talk to someone about adoption." I'm not sure what we were anticipating—commiseration, pity—but the woman just smiled and said, "Hold on a minute." Then we were ushered into a waiting room and told that someone would be down to talk with us shortly.

Once the lady had closed the door behind her, Chris turned to me and said, "I think she would have told us if the waiting list were still closed, don't you?"

"Yes," I assured her, "I do." I knew how Chris felt from the urgency in her voice.

Please God, let the waiting list be open this time, I prayed. I didn't know how Chris would handle another rejection, for that is how it seemed to us, that we were being rejected as parents without being given even the slightest chance. We hadn't entirely accepted adoption as an alternative for raising a family, but we had ruled out any others we had learned about. And this was our last attempt. Chris had said, 'Three times and you're out.' And she had meant it. If the waiting list was still closed after a year of waiting and two previous attempts to get on it, then our future as a childless couple would be decided.

The door was opened quietly and a woman whom we had remembered from our first visit a year ago greeted us warmly.

"Hello," she said and shook our hands in turn. "Niall and Christine, isn't it? I'm Helen Clancy. How are you?"

We followed her up a flight of stairs and into a cheerful

room. As soon as we were seated, Chris turned to her and asked, "Is the waiting list open?"

"Yes," Helen replied. "I would have phoned you, but I didn't have your number. It opened in October."

Over cups of strong tea we talked a little about adoption. We explained that we weren't one hundred percent sure about adopting a baby. Helen said she was glad to hear us voice our doubts. Over the course of the next year we would discover together whether or not adoption was for us and on behalf of St. Catherine's, Helen would help us. She asked us to take the application home, think it over again, and return it to her if we wanted to proceed further.

We left thinking at least we had a choice now. If we decided to go ahead and if we were approved as 'adoptive parents', there would be a little baby out there somewhere waiting for us. Chris filled out the initial application the next day and sent it in to Helen.

And so, that thread of hope—the hope that one day we might adopt a baby—also ran through all the dark mornings and sudden evenings of winter. The cows moved down out of the hill fields and lingered along the walls around the back of the house, nosing the cold stones and crunching hoofprints in the frosted grass. Spring seemed impossibly far off. The word that foxes had been seen at night went quickly about our townland. The old red timber door to the hens' cabin had to be doubly secured, tied and chained. The hunger of winter was birds at the berry bushes and night mice at the hens' meal bag. Set traps, put out poison, I was told, and said I would, knowing full well that there was something in all this minutely struggling winter life that I couldn't quite bring myself to kill. Here in Kiltumper, it seemed to me, we were all part of it together.

It was the small not the great moments of life here that formed this farm, that linked the world of the animals ineluctably to our hearts, and made us aware of the innumerable threads tying man, land and beast together into a whole.

Helen phoned yesterday to say that she was coming to visit us next week. God, what will she think of our home? I looked at everything with an inspector's eye, imagining her examining everything, peering into cupboards and corners. Well, I can easily clean those, but there's not much I can do about the floor coverings. One of these days we'll be able to get a carpet for the parlor and the bathroom and new lino for the back kitchen. She won't hold that against us. After all it *is* a *farm* house. But the settee in the kitchen, the main room of the cottage, is disgraceful, the leatherette is cracked and peeling. How can I expect her not to notice that! Well, there's only one thing to be done — re-cover it. I called Lucy. She said she and Tessie are old hands at reupholstery and would be up tomorrow first thing, meanwhile I was to go out and buy the material. So I spent the evening with a little screwdriver prising out the million staples holding the shabby old red vinyl covering in place. Tomorrow, it will look brand new and then anyone would be delighted to sit upon so fine a settee and sip a cup of tea and nibble at a biscuit and chat about any little old thing—like adoption.

Of our four cows, Bridget, a "tidy" three-year-old Simmental, had not come in calf. Through the previous July and August she had had the bull three times, and still not become pregnant. "Her cycle could be off, Crissie," Mary advised. "She could have been bulled the first time too young, you know," said another of our neighbors, Michael Dooley, as we sat in his house around the fire, enjoying delicious scones baked by Breda, his wife. "Now she's bulling every six weeks or so, ye wouldn't know how she'd be. Ye'd be best off to sell her," he said at last, bringing a sudden air of harsh reality to the little enterprise of our farm.

Of course, it went without saying, that we didn't want to sell her. Although in the beginning we had promised each other that we would not form attachments to the cows, that we would see them and their calves as a crucial part of our yearly budget, money we needed for our survival, arguments and reasoning were hopeless now. The cows were our family and Bridget was Chris's favorite cow. Last year, she had named Bridget's first and only calf—the calf which came with Bridget when we bought her—Lemondrop. Chris became even more attached to Bridget as we delayed doing anything about her, pushing the problem further and further into the winter. As the great black bellies of the other cows began to balloon up with life, and their steps across the fields became ever more slow and matronly, Bridget trotted like a sadness after them. Sometimes, as the three other ladies rested themselves on the little crest of a hill, the Simmental drifted off by herself, grazing the far corners in a kind of still dream. Afternoons and evenings Chris would go out to look at her.

"She makes me so sad. It's crazy, I know, but I can't help thinking that she *knows* the others have calves inside them, and she doesn't." I was afraid to ask what else Chris might be thinking that would make her sad—I suppose I knew without asking.

"I know," I said, knowing, too, that despite everything we simply had to sell her and replace her with another in-calf heifer. If we didn't we'd have only three calves next year. And to put it bluntly, we couldn't afford it.

For a couple of weeks, winter fell around us and closed off all decision; the fields were frozen hard and crisp and it was unsuitable weather for the sale of a cow. Bridget stayed, fattening toward spring. Then, on a mild day in February a man arrived at the back gate; he bought animals for fattening I was told. How he'd heard of Bridget I don't know, but he was here and he was interested in her. Leaving Chris in the kitchen I pulled on my Wellies and followed him out over the back wall to view her, a great wordless lump in my throat. With his hands behind his back, he scrutinized her in the middle distance, then edged nearer until he got his hand on her rump. With a little giddy frisk, Bridget trotted away.

"She's in grand form," he said to me.

"She is," I said.

"I'll give you four hundred for her."

I paused. The air was clear and cold and our breaths steamed quietly in the middle of the big field. I didn't want to be doing this.

"Fine," I said, and there and then took the money.

Within half an hour Bridget was herded down to the cabin, separated from the others, and loaded into the back of a cattle lorry. She bellowed briefly as she clattered up the walkway, and then, with the rattle of the little chain locks and the banging of a hand on the back to make certain all was secure, she was taken away. The goat, who had followed her all the way down to the cabin, was left out in the road by herself when the lorry disappeared. Chris went toward her, but in a flash, the goat turned and clattered away down the road and found her own way back to the remainder of our little herd.

Several times in midwinter and early spring Helen in her little white car headed out from Ennis and bumped around the ribbon roads of west Clare to come and meet with us in Kiltumper. The marked days on the calendar on which she was due were like stepping-stones to spring. She sat in the kitchen for cups of coffee, and, nestled together under gray skies, we were three people in a room talking about pain and loss and hope and an imaginary child. These were hard days but hopeful days, days in which emotion was sometimes bottled tight and then, quite unexpectedly, spilled over.

Sitting in the big airy room upstairs in St. Catherine's for our first group meeting with ten other couples who wished to adopt, I felt the weight of unspoken emotions in the silence, the shared, muted grieving so tinged with a feeling of personal failure, and the great welling of hope. The distant sounds of Ennis traffic were the background. There was a desperate longing to wave wands through the air, banish this obstacle to life, explain the unexplainable, and reason out why anyone longing to do so should be unable to have children. But instead, we sat tight, husbands and wives holding their teacups and looking down into the worn nap of the carpet while Father Geoghegan, the head of St. Catherine's, spoke.

It was the start of a long slow process of healing. In a way, for Chris and me, it began to seem integral to our whole decision to move to the west of Ireland; we had given up one life to adopt another, and in that, we imagined, was prefigured the vast dimensions of adoption itself, the trials and rewards, the completely unknowable way ahead. On still days, as we waited for Helen to come or watched her drive away down the Kiltumper road, we often thought that this, perhaps, had been the latent but predestined reason for our having come here in the first place. For here was something we hadn't and couldn't have imagined as we had rushed around our offices in Manhattan, where we had foreseen for ourselves the fairly typical shape of family life. How we might have lived and coped with childlessness in the anxious, office-bound, pressure-cooker atmosphere of New York, we cannot say. And yet, more and more, as we walked our feelings out over the fields of Upper and Lower Tumper, it came to seem to both of us that Kiltumper was the place we were meant to be, and that it was here that we were meant to start our family, by adopting a child.

But . . .

Nothing was certain yet. At the end of the first group meeting, forms were handed out.

"Get these filled in by your employers, and get them back to us as soon as possible," said Father Geoghegan, "then we can take care of all the paperwork side of things. They're just statements to certify that you are employed, and capable of supporting a child, and so on. They're nothing to worry about," he said and then saw that we looked worried. "Of course, I forgot, if you're self-employed you just get a statement from your bank manager to the effect that you are financially solvent. All right?"

We nodded, all right. And walked down the stairs with the others, feeling a terrible sinking sensation. How could any bank manager say we were "financially solvent?" We lived in Kiltumper on the tightest budget imaginable, growing vegetables in the garden and tending the hens and chickens not just for the fun of it, but because we needed to. We literally counted on every penny made from the calves and the annual sale of hay. Our bank balance, although never in the red, just barely stayed in the black.

That evening, back in the cottage, the winter seemed darker and quieter than ever. We had already envisaged the possibility of not being approved for adoption on emotional or psychological grounds. Now to these was added the extra obstacle of money. It seemed a cruel irony that we had given up well-paying jobs in Manhattan because, among other things, we had dreamed of raising a family in Ireland.

For a few days we did nothing. We folded the form for the bank manager and left it on the kitchen dresser. Then, at five o'clock one evening the phone rang. I picked it up and recognized at once the faint crackle and echo of an overseas call.

"Hello, is this Niall Williams and Christine Breen of Kiltumper?"

"Yes, it is," I said. "This is Niall."

"Hello," said the man's voice, speaking from three thousand miles away. He introduced himself as president of a New York publishing company, and then added, quite casually, "I'd like to publish your book."

Even as I heard it, I was nodding and hand-signaling the news to Chris at my side. This was news that would change the shape of our lives once more, and might make it possible for us to adopt a baby. It couldn't possibly have come at a better time. Ten minutes later, I put down the phone. My hands were shaking. "We'll get the contracts right away," I said, "and an advance!"

"Yipee!" yelled Chris.

"Financially solvent!" I shouted, as we did a little jig dance together in the kitchen.

Moments later, we were outside, walking our familiar walk in a landscape on the very edge of spring, to the fields of Tumper to shout the news. Up there that day the wind suddenly seemed warmer than before, thin blades of new grass were growing, the drains (ditches) rushed with water. It wouldn't be long now until the gorse bloomed and the blackthorns were all white with blossom. Suddenly we could see the coming greens and golds of spring and summer sweep over us. It wouldn't be long now.

Standing on the wall, watching us pass, the black goat bleated twice.

"*She could be very lucky for ye,*" I could hear Mary say.

CHAPTER TWO

We were on the waiting list. It was an enormous step, and yet, for the time being, it landed us nowhere. We were still on that anxious middle ground, and as the early spring days passed by we thought and rethought the whole thing a thousand times. There were evenings when doubts over-rode everything, when the rampant imaginings of a child in the house seemed so all-encompassing that there would be time for little else. There were moments when we sincerely doubted our own ability as prospective parents, and swam in a sea of worries about the whole business of adopting. Should we, shouldn't we; it was like tottering on the edge of a precipice. We continually thought it over. At one moment we were ambivalent about changing what had, after all, just become a settled new life-style. Would we have time to do the very things we had come here for? But in the end we were swept up by our wish to have a baby. It seemed crucial to our happiness. We moved around the house and the farm tense with waiting for Helen Clancy to call.

Helen was a kind of light to us in the next year of our lives. She is a lovely, gentle woman with shining eyes and a smile that was full of understanding. She became our partner in this, a kind of midwife between our worries and dreams as we were being assessed for approval as adoptive parents and the actuality.

Adoption in Ireland works like this: Over all, there is the Adoption Board in Dublin. It's the government-appointed body for all the individual adoption societies around the country, like St. Catherine's. In our case, we went on a waiting list, and while we were "waiting," Helen visited us several times in our home and got to know us and the reasons why we wanted to adopt. During that time she assessed and evaluated us to determine if we would make good parents. If we were approved, a baby would then be placed with us sometime within two years from the date we'd applied.

Chris was worried that because she was an American the Irish Adoption Board might not want to consider our application. But as she was married to an Irish citizen, and as we had been living here a couple of years and had established residency, the fact of her American citizenship would make little difference, Helen said. Adoption societies in Ireland get tons of letters from couples in the United States wanting to adopt Irish babies, but unfortunately, it is not possible to adopt a baby in Ireland unless you actually live here.

"What age will the baby be?" Chris asked during one of our first at-home meetings with Helen.

Helen replied, "We try to place babies within the first six months of the baby's life, but you never know. A baby could be older because the mother might have decided later to give her baby to us to be adopted. Generally, the babies we place are around three months old and, until the time that they are placed with adoptive parents, they will have been cared for by a foster mother."

"That sounds good to me," said Chris.

"Do you want a *little* baby, Christine?" Helen asked.

"Oh, yes," Chris replied, "as young as possible." She paused. Helen was looking at her, waiting for more. "I want to hear that newborn cry they make when they're tiny, tiny," she said. Helen smiled.

"What else is in store?" I asked, knowing that there was more to it then the magic of a newborn's cry.

"After we place the baby with you there is a period of six months, sometimes longer, even up to a year, when the baby is with you but not legally yours. It's a trial period. During that time you can give the baby back, or the baby's natural mother can take the baby back. It doesn't happen very often, but it does happen and I can't guarantee that it won't happen to you." Chris and I looked at each other. The whole process lay spread before us, labyrinthine, complex, full of pitfalls and risk.

"It's best not even to think about it," Helen said. "We try our best to see that kind of thing coming and, as I said, it hardly ever happens. But occasionally it does and you just have to bear that in mind."

We learned further that during the six-month trial period, the natural mother has the right to reclaim her baby at a moment's notice. Even up to the final day when we would be called to Dublin to the Adoption Board for the legal transfer of the baby to us, the natural mother would have a right to take her baby back.

But, as Helen cautioned us, it was something to think about but not to dwell on. The adoption process in Ireland has evolved steadily over the years and many happy babies have been placed with many happy couples. In fact, everyone's interests are considered—the natural mother's, most of all.

"Her decision has to be the right one for her and for the baby, and it is the job of the Adoption Society to counsel the mother and not to persuade her," said Helen. "For example," she added, "in some cases the natural mother wants to meet the prospective parents. How would you feel about that?"

We were both taken aback. It was something we had not expected to be asked and seemed very unusual to us. Helen sensed our surprise and said, "It's okay, you know. It's not necessary. A lot of couples don't want to meet the natural mother."

"Oh, no," said Chris immediately, "I think it's a good idea. I just hadn't thought about it before." Helen nodded.

In the weeks ahead, we were asked more difficult questions, questions that required honest answers, questions that forced both of us to consider the moral and social as well the emotional aspects of adoption. And meeting the mother was certainly something we had to think about.

It would all be a long, anxious wait, but one that could result in a family. For the moment, however, we couldn't allow ourselves to hope too much. In the event that we weren't approved we would have to live with that too. For, if there was one thing we had been taught so far, it was acceptance. Now we could look to spring with new eyes. Chris was full of fresh ideas for the garden, new paintings had been planned, we were writing a first play together, and busy keeping our Kiltumper journals. In the back meadow our cows were all due to calf. The newness of another springtime was upon us.

Another April first and our third April in Ireland. We're heading into our third summer and it better be a good one this year. Daffodils and primroses brighten up the dark earth outside the kitchen window and the rest of the garden is coming sluggishly alive. Today I sprinkled some bonemeal around the plants that are pushing their way up and, having read somewhere that chicken manure was high in nitrogen and great for the garden, I sprinkled some of that, too, from a pile of it I mixed with turf dust that I had been saving to use as compost for the flower borders. The things you can learn. When I think of the things I *have* learned since coming to Ireland . . . I could make a list of them that would fill a book! From using spent chicken manure in the garden to boiling the kettle on the open fire, from baking brown bread scones to dehorning calves, from "footing" turf to "earthing up" potatoes, from designing sets for the drama group to fattening turkeys. And painting, in itself, has been quite a learning process too. Like everything else, it takes time. Discoveries come slowly. Today I'm thinking ahead to my summer paintings of the garden, of all the flowers there will be—like colors on my palette—of fine weather and cobalt skies.

But, silently, I'm listening for a baby.

Our cows were in calf. Their bellies big as barrels, they moved slowly now across the back meadow. Hugely swollen matrons of our farm, their pregnancies had gathered, filled, and almost overtaken them in the early days of spring. They were enormously rounded. Each morning as they made their way heavily across the fields to the iron feeder where I cut and forked the silage, I looked at them like a nervous midwife. Here, after all, were to be the profits of our farming year—the calves, our yield. We were in the business of rearing beef calves; we had gone through the previous summer with three or four daily inspections to catch each cow coming "bulling," or in heat; we had brought Michael's Hereford bull up the road a half-dozen times to service them, and watched and waited the days to see if each beast was in calf. So that the farming, the *husbanding* of the animals through the winter, had taken on special meaning for us. For months we had hardly believed they were in calf and that a day in spring would come when we would see our own livestock being born here. And yet, each morning in the early frost or mist, traipsing out across the field to fork out the feed, I looked upon four cows more caringly than I had imagined possible. In a peculiar sort of way we had become attached to each other; we were mutually dependent parts of the farm. And damn it, I have to say it, we *liked* these cows.

Counting from the day each cow was bulled, Chris had figured the nine months to their calving dates. Susie was first, due on the fourth of April. A few days before her due date I asked Michael to walk out into the field with me and take a look. Moving quietly up to her, he had reached out his hand to feel her hip. In an instant his hand brushed her back and she kicked and hurried away from us, trotting briskly all the way to the far corner of the meadow. In that instant he had made his judgment. "She's not ready, Niall. She'll be a few days yet," he said, scrutinizing the others and lighting up his cigarette. "They're in fine form, God bless 'em," he added. "Are they?" I said, gazing at them with a flush of pride.

April 4 came and went. Still no calf. We took turns making checks on Susie, and for a week saw no signs. It is almost impossible to describe how large an event this calving had become in our minds. Each day was filled with it. We slept nights with a window open, thinking we would hear Susie's bellowing if she went into labor, and we woke in the mornings to look quickly out into the back field for the newborn calf, hoping that as we slumbered in the darkness a calf had quietly, easily been born. Of course, the fear that there would be complications and the calf would die being born went unspoken. Ten months earlier I had seen a short farm video on calving difficulties, but now, facing the real thing, I could only recollect vague blood-and-mucus images, burst afterbirths, and strangulated newborns. For a week we had a cabin readied, swept, disinfected, and newly lain with dry bedding. We had bought cow chains, new buckets for water, and fixed the cabin lights. Still, no calf.

Then, almost exactly one week after her calving date, it began. Chris had noticed a change in her, and Michael was called into the back field again. Again we crept up on her, and again he reached his hand onto her hip before she hurried off. "She's ready now all right, Crissie," he announced. "She'll calf today." By nightfall though, there was still no sign of labor. Following instructions, we brought Susie down for the night to the calving cabin. Water and hay were laid on in abundance. The light was left burning. We were to check her every three hours for the rest of the night.

Eleven o'clock. Nothing. No sign. Unless perhaps she seemed to be sweating heavily. Was the cabin too hot for her? Was she running a fever? Should we open a window?

There was no water in her trough. Refilling it, we went to bed and, fitfully, tried to sleep. At one o'clock, unable to sleep or wait the agreed three-hour interval, we rose, pulled on Wellingtons and went out to check her in our pajamas.

She was breathing heavily. Her eyes were wild looking and a thin loop of lucent stuff dangled from her rear. I tried to remember whether it should be there or not, and couldn't. For almost an hour we watched her, standing inside the cabin door in our coats and pajamas in the absolute quiet of night. And then, it happened.

From somewhere within the giant barrel of her insides, there was a heave, an enormous pushing that spouted for a single moment and brought a glimpse of white hoof out through the mucus. It came and was gone, lost back inside her. Not knowing what to do or say, we said the kind of things people said in books or in movies. "Easy girl, easy now, good girl now, push, push!"

And believe it or not, she pushed. The white hoof flashed out again, an inch further. There was a deep loud sucking sound from within her, as dumbly the cow turned her head to us and then roared. Murmuring to her, patting her side and laying fresh hay beneath her, we watched on. Within half an hour the calf's legs had appeared. Slimed and black and shiny, they stuck out into the air fragile and crude. But were they the forelegs or the hind? Suddenly, the cabin seemed hot and close as I remembered fragmented details of breech births; if they were the hind legs, the calf could be in trouble, she could be locked at the hip, could suffocate in moments. Or so I seemed to remember, touching those twin hoofs and trying to picture them: fore or hind legs? Any farmer would know at once, of course. But me? I couldn't decide. The labor, it seemed, had stopped altogether now. There was no more pushing. I was alarmed. "I'm sure she's all right," said Chris, "but go down and get Michael if you think you should."

It was difficult to do, to disturb someone in the middle of the night and ask him to come up and help you with your cow and your calf. And yet, it was part of the very first lesson we had learned since moving here from Manhattan: neighbors are friends, are sharers in the same endeavor to make a living from a farm. Helping was a part of the life-style. Farms that bounded each other necessarily brought farmers into each other's lives in one way or another. So, pulling on a sweater and jeans over my pajamas, I got into the old Peugeot and drove to Downeses. The house was in darkness, the seven little children sleeping. Around to the back window in the cold half-moonlight I crept, feeling like a dawn rebel surreptitiously stirring the troops. I tapped on the window twice. Michael's head rose up in the shadow.

"Hello?"

"She's calving, Michael. I think she might be having trouble," I whispered loudly against the cool glass of the windowpane.

"I'll be right there," said Michael, shaking himself from the bed. By the time, moments later, that I saw his tousled head coming out the front door, I was already feeling sorry that I had woken him. Yet, in the way he had about him, climbing into the car, he made me feel at once that the bother was nothing.

"Crissie up, Niall?" he asked, as I sped the car back along the dark potholed road to the cow cabin.

"Yes, she's been up with me."

"Oh!" he said, comically rolling his eyes at the great fuss we were making.

At the cabin he got out of the car and walked over to Chris standing in the light of the doorway.

"Lovely night, Mrs. Williams!" he said with a grin, and with that stepped inside to take a look.

We watched him anxiously. The birthing had progressed no further and still the two legs projected stiffly out into the air. The cow had begun to foam at the mouth. "I couldn't tell if they were the front legs . . ." I began, trying to explain. "They are, all right, Niall," said Michael patting the cow along her back and taking a step away from her. "What do you think, Michael?" asked Chris from the door. "Everything's absolutely spot on, so it is," he said. "No panic." Then, turning to me, he casually asked, "Any bit of an old rope around, Niall?"

Old rope and fresh water. Susie turned her head in the chain and bellowed to us. She slurped up three buckets of water in moments while Michael attached the rope to the calf's forelegs. The cow was pushing again, the great bellows of her insides blowing and sucking, as we took the rope and readied to pull. "When I say *now*, Niall," were my instructions. For a second we were all three tightly concentrated there in that warm little cabin in the middle of the night. I was tense as a fighter.

"*Now*, Niall, pull!"

And we pulled and the calf surged forward and with a slipping squeezing opening motion its head appeared, pressed down upon the extended legs, like a diver headed out to sea. Its eyes and mouth were closed lifelessly.

"Now. Again, pull!"

This time it came free to the hip, this fragile black and shiny beast, coated in slime and water. It hung there half from the cow in a kind of horrible midlife until "NOW!" the final pull came, and with that the calf was tugged clean out onto the floor. It smacked down onto the hay solidly, and it seemed to Chris and me that it was surely dead.

Michael had already leapt to it.

"It's a black whitehead heifer," he announced to us as if

we were the proud parents. Then, gathering her up in his arms he tucked her over into the corner beneath Susie's head and we waited for the mother to begin caressing her newborn, to stroke life into her calf with her big, warm tongue. But Susie just looked at us and did nothing. Immediately Michael took up a piece of straw and plunged it into the calf's nostrils to let in air. The calf breathed, but its mother ignored it. Still chained to the wall, Susie moved about in fright and innocence and nearly trampled her calf several times.

"Watch it!"

"Easy there, easy!"

"Stop that now, stop that," said Michael in a firm voice, bending beneath the cow's udder and starting to draw the all-important and immunity-building first milk, or beastings. We heard it before we saw it, the steady squirt of white liquid jetting out over the stone floor. With Michael's hand still on the udder, the trembling, cooling body of the calf was lifted into the line of the milk. It ran across her lips. She licked at it, and then at last raised her head to suck.

"There you are now. No panic, Niall," said Michael, standing back with us at the cabin door. We three stood together watching the calf suckling. We watched and watched, without saying a word. Then Michael came into the house and drank a cup of coffee with Chris and me. We sat there together, three people in the middle of the night, feeling the shared satisfaction of the first calf born on this farm for years. There was a deep glowing warmth in the kitchen, a joy that would inform the days of spring ahead of us, and the birthing of two more calfs.

It was a beautiful day in the month of May. It was a summerlit noon time in Kiltumper that neither of us

31

would forget for the rest of our lives. We were in the garden. The front door was open. Away to the south the green patterned fields of Hayes' farm shone, lustrous in the sunshine. On the road to the village nobody came or went and the whole of the west Clare countryside seemed held, hushed by the tremendous promise of early summer. Somewhere in the midst of the flower garden Chris was weeding. I was tired, standing with a fork above ridges of potatoes that were yet to be cast, or earthed up. I was watching the still, absolutely motionless figures of four horses in the farthest field from us when suddenly, from inside the house, the phone rang.

"Niall, will you get it?" Chris asked.

In my Wellingtons I hurried into our kitchen and lifted the phone.

"Hello, is this Niall?"

"Helen, how are you?" I said, looking out the window to where Chris was kneeling, weeding patiently along the front path where the arabis spilled over. It was Helen calling from St. Catherine's. My heart started racing. I could barely catch my breath.

"I'm fine thanks, Niall," she said. "Niall, I just wanted to phone and let you know the good news. You've just been approved."

Approved. The waiting was over. We were going to become parents after all. We had been approved!

"Of course, you'll receive official word by post in the next day or two. I just wanted to let you and Chris know. It'll probably be Christmas before anything now. I'll be in touch. Congratulations. Bye."

I walked out into that noontime stillness of the garden and surrounding countryside not knowing how to tell it. It had happened so quickly, much faster than we had expected. Chris looked up from the flowers.

"Who was it?"

"It was Helen," I said and blurted it out. "We've been approved for the adoption. We're going to have a baby by Christmas."

For a tiny flickering moment she simply looked to me, her face in the sunlight there above the flowers. One instant. Then she smiled, dropped her head and burst into tears.

Mayday. Babyday. A baby *is* coming our way. Not the usual way, maybe, but baby will come our way, anyway. A stork, thinly disguised as a social worker, will bring him or her, Sean or Deirdre, the names we have already chosen, to us. If it's a girl, we're going to name her Deirdre May Williams. Sort of Irish with an American twist. (I wonder, though, about Sean May Williams.)

Mayday. The first day of Irish summer. The first day of the farm year when the fresh grass starts growing and when hay still left in the haggard is a sign of good husbandry. Well, we still have silage for feeding our cows over beyond the haybarn, so we must be doing something right.

Mayday. Maybough. Traditional time for gathering a branch of whitethorn or yellow furze and Mayflowers in celebration of a fine summer to come. For us, on this first day of May, we celebrate being 'approved' as adoptive parents. I should fill the house with buttercups, cowslips, and bluebells, and whitethorn and furze boughs galore. In fact, maybe we should name the baby, Whitethorn, like a little Indian. Now that's American!

Bealtaine, the month of May. This time last year we were almost leaving here. The weather had almost beaten us and in the days of wet summer I had found myself thinking of Gaelic words, old sounds that in some ways seemed to catch exactly the roughness, harshness, of our condition itself. *Fliuch* meaning wet, *baisteach* meaning rain, between those two sounds we had squelched all summer. There was something in them that kept coming back at me. "*Fliuch,*" I would mutter to myself going up across soft fields and boggy places and letting out the sound like a curse. "*Fliuch.*" It was flowing and harsh in the same moment; it was cold rain on windy days, ceaselessly veiling the horizon. It was the word for that summer.

And now, in this year's Maytime, *i mBealtaine,* crossing the dry meadow in the sunshine, there sprang up a whole new series of the old Irish words. They had come to seem like utterances of the landscape itself to me, something I had all but lost, a language made up almost entirely of the sculpted sounds of wind and light, sun and rain along a lonely western roadway. These days were lovely, *ailainn, tirim agus teo,* dry and warm. I sometimes sounded those words aloud, with the greatest of happiness. Our lives were looking up, we thought. Here in Kiltumper we felt like people who had come through, and hiking up across the bog and feeling the spring of turf underfoot, I let back my head to laugh out loud. The sun was on my back, and all the day long was *tirim, teo, agus ailainn*.

CHAPTER
THREE

I was hurrying across the fields, heading up Tumper under a sky so blue I might have dreamed it. I expected the animals to be in the upper field and, as I went in search of them, I was climbing towards a view that stretches all the way westwards to the glinting ocean. What a day it was! It quickened my pulse and gladdened my heart.

I was in the field a few minutes before I realized the cows and their calves were gone. In a flash I saw our early morning plans for a day at the seaside vanish.

We had awakened early to the quiet shimmering of fabulous sunlight. The drumming, blowing racket of rain against windows was gone, and hurrying from the quiet, cavelike bedroom with its three-foot-thick walls we had rushed out to the garden to see the sky. It was a beautiful day. Summer had arrived. Everything seemed to rise and stretch in the sunshine and the warm colors of Chris's flower garden danced gaily down the path. There were no clouds anywhere. Way across the view to the south the fields dazzled deeply green. The rush of warmth into the air made everything seem giddy with life.

Almost at once Chris had been seized with plans. There were a thousand things to do on a day like this (and chasing after cows was not one of them). Should she go out with her easel and oils, had she a canvas ready? No. Rather, we had decided to go to the sea at once, pack a picnic, bring books, towels, swimsuits. It was a summer holiday.

"I'll feed the hens and chickens, you check the cows and calves," she had said, and we had bustled about the kitchen in sunstruck panic.

But they were all gone, cows and calves. There wasn't a sign of them anywhere. Not within the bounds of the field, nor of the one below it. Where could they have gotten to? The whole herd was lost. I began to hurry along by the stone walls, peering into the green distance where every stone whitened in the sunlight might have been a calf. No. Nothing. No sign of them. I doubled back and looked again. Having heard of animals sometimes falling into a drain, I slid down into the open drain by Melican's bounds and hurried along it. No tracks, no hoofprints. Again, I went back up the hill to stare across the full farm and off into our neighbors' lands. I must have been gone for an hour when I saw Chris coming up across the fields to find me.

"What's happened?"

"The cows are gone."

We split up to search for them. Chris went west into the next farm and I went towards the bog, my mind filled with dread as I remembered tales of cattle sunk into the wet softnesses of the turfland. Were we to be known hereafter, I wondered, as the farmers who lost their entire herd to the bog? I walked out around the banks of stacked turf and along the wide drain that separates the top meadow from the bog.

Chris found the animals. They had crossed the stone wall at a low corner and traveled the breadth of our neighbor's lands to settle in amongst his cattle. While I was crossing and recrossing the bog, Chris was moving between forty beasts with a short elderberry branch, trying to separate out our cows. As I came back down the hill, I picked her out. That she was there at all, single-handedly, patiently turning cows from bullocks seemed a marvel to me when only a year previously both of us would have run from a single trotting cow. I caught up to her as she drove them through the gap back onto our land.

"I couldn't find Gerty," she said.

"Are you sure?" There was panic in my voice.

"Yes. She wasn't there."

"Her two calves?" I asked as I quickly counted our little herd.

"They're here."

It made no sense. Normally the mother wouldn't stray far from her calves. We both knew enough to know that, and for the second time that morning we set out to search. Something was not right.

For two more hours of that blue sunlit day we walked back and forth searching every corner of a hundred acres. In the end hopelessness rose over us and I went back down the road to Michael to ask for help.

"You can't find her?" he said. "Well Niall, she must be there somewhere. Don't panic, we'll find her all right. Peter and Francie!"

The boys were called and in a moment slipped from their Sunday clothes into jeans and Wellingtons. With lengths of stiff black rubber piping for their sticks, they stood by the door and looked to me.

"Cow gone missing, Niall?" said Francie, with a broad smile from ear to ear.

"Cow gone missing, Francie," I said, without so much as a grin at all.

That beautiful warm day in June was the finest day of the year. There were five of us, and the size of our force lessened my dread that we would not find her. And yet I walked up Tumper with very mixed emotions, feeling both relieved and foolish. Here we were after all, dragging Michael from his cup of tea and his Sunday paper because *one of our cows was lost*. It was bumbling and amateurish. I couldn't imagine it happening to anyone else. But Michael whistled happily as we moved through the cows and calves. "No panic, Niall," he said, "Peter and Francie, go down along Sean's bounds there and up along by the bog meadow. Quick now."

West Clare cowboys, they galloped away over the hilltop on imaginary horses while Michael, Chris, and I headed up into the bog. Through the uncut meadow Michael had followed Gerty's tracks, had glimpsed the brushed, flattened grass and the green meandering path along which, for perhaps no reason in the world, she had decided to set off and wander into the dawn.

Gerty, Bossy Gerty, Broody Gerty, Big Gerty, Old Gerty. We knew her personality and foibles. We knew how she refused to let her calves suckle, kicking and turning from them until the moment when *she* wished to be milked, how she led the herd, and sometimes head-charged the younger animals if they went toward the gate before her. We knew her ladylike trot, her massive bellow, the very look in her eye when she caught us coming, and her mixture of pride and wariness as we daily inspected the two very fine bullocks she was rearing at the giant balloons of her udders.

Cursing under our breath, we followed her trail into the

bog. She had gone into the drain and for as far as Chris and I marched by its side we could find no hoofprints to show where she had come out. The sun was high and the fabulous day was spinning past us. Three hours had passed already since I had left the house filled with anticipation of our picnic by the sea to check the cows. Michael had stopped whistling. Across the horizon Peter and Francie were slowly coming towards us. There was no sign of her. In those silent Sunday morning moments as each of us stood there, staring about in all directions, I felt an overwhelming sense of our littleness in all of this. We had been found out. We had lost the animal and felt that loss not only in the sense of her worth but as the intrusion of reality upon a dream. I cannot emphasize this enough. That moment, more than the weather, or any of the hardships we had faced since coming here, meant defeat to us.

And then, Chris found her.

"There she is!"

Her cry was composed of everything: struggle, failure, endurance, and victory. There Gerty was. There, a long way across the brown, empurpled expanse of the bogland, up beyond the barbed wire that ringed the pine-tree forestry, we could just make out the black and white shape of her head. She had sunk into the bog.

"That's her all right, Crissie," said Michael quietly, standing there, lighting his cigarette and thinking what to do.

"She's sunk in," I said, unable to refrain from stating the obvious.

"She is, I'd say," Michael agreed.

"Will we be able to get her out, Michael?" Chris asked after a moment.

"Oh, we will, Crissie, no panic," he said. And we were off.

As we hurried closer the full extent of the problem

became apparent to us. Gerty had blundered into a quaggy wet corner of the bog and instantly sunk to her hips. Now, bellowing to us as we approached, her great black body tried to shift and rise, but it was hopeless. Her legs were sunk beneath her, and with every effort a deep wet sucking sound squelched out of the bog as she heaved. Finally, she lay there unable to move. Peter and Francie reached her first. "Leave her a minute," shouted Michael to them. Turning to Chris and me, he said, "She might rise out of it herself, you know, when she sees us coming." Again she bellowed and Chris's heart went out to her, the lamed beast, the fallen mother, roaring out of the very bellows of nature to be freed, to be back once again with her calves. We forgot our anger at her. Stepping carefully in a circle around her, Michael tested the ground, stamping his boot. We felt the whole spongy softness of the bog, quivering.

Gerty was wild with panic. Her great brown watery eyes rolled to each of us, back and forth.

"She might rise out of it, Niall, if we could frighten her," said Michael. And with that, we all began to cry and yell, Peter, Francie, Chris, Michael, and I all roaring and waving our hands like crazy, until we were breathless. There we were, five people on a summerlit day, jumping and shouting at a frightened cow in the middle of a desolate brown bog. And by now it was afternoon.

The cow didn't, couldn't, stand. Our voices died away on the air. "Give me that," said Michael to Francie, taking from him the short rubber pipe. "Niall, take one of those," he said, his voice suddenly a shade more urgent. "She won't get out of it, we'll have to try this. Give her a good belt now." And with that his arm rose and fell through the air, whacking down on the cow's hide. I was stunned at the force of the blow, and was still in shock as a second crashed down on her. Within a moment, I had joined in. We had to terrify her more than the terror of the bog itself. The blows rained down on her. Peter and Francie stood silently by, Chris turned away. I was sweating and sickened with it, crying out and thrashing at the poor cow as spurts of red blood rose from her black hide. Her back became ridged with welts as she rocked and bellowed to get up. Massive sucking sounds spluttered wetly up from beneath her, opening even wider the ground into which she had sunk. Her mouth foamed, her head fell to one side with exhaustion. We dropped our rods and walked back from her.

"Peter and Francie, get her some water in something, look, one of those bags. Quick now."

Michael lit a cigarette. For a moment the three of us stood there beneath the perfectly blue sky and said nothing. Down at his home, Michael's Sunday dinner would already be cooked. Already men and women would be heading off on afternoon *cuairds* or visits, or down to Kilmihil to watch the football match.

"Crissie," said Michael at last, "go as far as Sean's and ask him to come up with the tractor and a bit of rope. Tell him she's right stuck over by the forestry."

We watched her go. I didn't know what to say. I wanted to apologize to Michael for taking so much of his time, I wanted to apologize for being a novice farmer and for letting Gerty escape, even though I had no idea of how or why she had left a green field for the grassless waste of the bog. I felt guilty and wrong. I stood there watching Chris's bright red shirt disappear over the horizon, feeling the beginnings of relief. With Sean, and a tractor, surely we would get Gerty out. But when Chris was gone, Michael slowly stamped out his cigarette, and turning to me with a cautious look, said, "You know, Niall, Sean could have a hard time getting the tractor in as far as the cow. That bog is desperate soft."

A sunken cow and a sinking tractor. The rest of the day

was spent there upon the bog in a flurry of activity and effort. The fine clear light of the afternoon came and faded. Pale patterns of skimming cloud rose up from the western horizon and passed slowly above us. The fields were in green shadow for a moment, and birds flickered from the trees as tractor wheels spun and an engine sputtered to drag Gerty from a hole. The rope around her forelegs tautened across twenty feet of the heathery bog. While Chris and I watched on, Sean and Michael passed signals, called out from tractor to cow, checking each moment of the rescue as inch by inch the muddied black hocks of the beast at last appeared above ground. She was saved!

On solid ground she stood at once, and when the rope was taken from her she headed off by herself down the pathway to wait by the gate that led in to her calves.

What were we to say to Michael and Sean? In our first year we had already learned something of the mutual trust and helpfulness that was shared between neighbors, and yet, as we tried to begin farming, we worried that we depended too much on their goodwill. What kind of nuisance had we been? I turned to begin my apologies and thanks.

"Thank you, Michael; thanks, Sean. I'm very sorry."

"Sure 'twas a thing of nothing, Niall," said Sean, cutting me off. "A thing of nothing."

"No panic, Crissie, right?" said Michael, letting out his cigarette smoke to conceal his expression of held-in laughter.

Our days and nights were flecked now with imaginings of a baby in Kiltumper. Since we'd first heard that we had been approved, we found it almost impossible to picture ourselves with a baby. And yet at other times, it seemed so real and immediate that we almost tiptoed with nervousness around the prospect of our parenthood. What was it going to be like? How should we prepare? Would it be a boy or a girl? A million such questions flitted through our minds every day until Helen telephoned once again.

"Well, have you been thinking about it?"

"Yes. All the time," said Chris. "One minute there's no baby and the next, there she's going to be, right here in the kitchen."

"You think it's going to be a girl?"

"Well, I *have* been thinking about a girl. I don't know why. But I want to build a doll house."

"How would you feel if *she* was to arrive even sooner than December?"

"Sooner? What do you mean? Like when? . . . November?"

"What about next month!"

"Next month!"

We couldn't believe it. The world seemed to rush forward and burst into a flood of light across the kitchen floor. We were aglow, illuminated with a kind of dazzling happiness.

"Next month, Niall!" Chris repeated.

"In a month!" I said weakly, not knowing whether joy would make me laugh or cry.

But nothing was definite yet. There was a mother somewhere out there who wanted her little daughter to be brought up by a loving couple in the heart of the countryside, but before she would make any decision she wanted to meet the adoptive parents. This much Helen explained to us over the phone. Would we agree to meet her? We thought about it and said that we certainly would.

The meeting was set for the following week at St. Catherine's, and over the course of those seven days Chris and I went through every possible aspect of the whole adoption process once again. On the one hand it would be marvelous to meet the mother of a child you adopted; you would have so much more to tell the child about her later on, and could paint a fuller picture for her of her background. On the other hand, we knew the meeting would be extremely difficult, for although we both deeply wanted to love and raise a child, we didn't want any mother to feel we were 'taking' her baby, or to pressure her in any way. We would be there simply to try and be ourselves, to say as openly and honestly as possible: this is what we are like, this is who are, we would love your baby. And then stand back and wait for a decision.

The morning of the meeting was overcast and cloudy. We drove to St. Catherine's in Ennis in a hush, and went upstairs to the big waiting room. What happened after that is fractured in memory with the feelings of raw pain. A lovely, tall, dark-haired woman came in with Helen beside her. She was dressed in a summery white and blue dress. She had been crying, and as we all sat down together in a small circle and Helen introduced us to each other using first names only, I knew that this was going to be one of the most difficult experiences of our lives. In an hour that was so raw with emotion that I can hardly bring myself even to begin to describe it, Chris and I spoke of why we wanted to adopt a baby, and Elizabeth, as we called her, spoke of the deep love she felt for the baby girl she had given birth to and the new loving home she wanted her to have. "Spoke," of course, is hardly the word, for it was an hour wet with the tears of all three of us, full of half-sentences and hopelessly inadequate words fading into silence. In some ways it was hard not to feel that we were predators. And as Chris said openly to Elizabeth, we were not claiming that we could raise her baby any better than she could, and Elizabeth seemed really to appreciate that. We told her we wanted her decision to be the right one for

45

her, but if she decided to place the baby with St. Catherine's for adoption, we would be overjoyed. Elizabeth's greatest concern was for the baby, whom she thought would be at a severe disadvantage being raised in a single parent family, Ireland being what it is. Chris clasped Elizabeth's hands in hers; we all held onto each other and there in that big empty room in Ennis tried in turns to say the things that were so unsayable.

"If it works out that we adopt her, is there anything . . ." Chris's voice trailed off. Elizabeth was looking directly at her.

"I'd like you to keep her name," she said softly. "I've named her Deirdre."

Deirdre. It was the very name we wanted. In the end, Elizabeth got up to go and the three of us embraced tightly. She left with Helen, and for a little while Chris and I sat there alone, exhausted, like the shells of ourselves.

The meeting had gone very well, Helen told us. But it would be another while before Elizabeth reached her decision. In any case Helen would wait until the highly charged emotions of the meeting had subsided before speaking with Elizabeth again. That way, Helen would be sure not to be pressing the adoption in any fashion, and any decision would be reached freely. And yet, for Chris and me, the baby suddenly seemed a real possibility. We had even seen photographs of her. We couldn't help ourselves. Everything was preparation. In our little cottage, we hurried about readying our place for a baby. The small room off the big bedroom was to become a nursery. It needed insulating and painting. There hadn't been a child raised in the cottage for over half a century, and in shaping a space for the baby the physical ancientness of the place sometimes seemed to collide with the ideal of modern baby rooms. Here the walls were three feet thick and rose crookedly fifteen feet to a timber-slatted ceiling where wind gusted down from the thin roof. Spiderwebs clung in high corners and the long flex of the single light bulb dangled from a dusty shade. The floor of poured cement had cracked in places, and the new inexpensive carpet we had bought to cover it seemed to rise and fall gently like the surface of a sea. With peach paint we daubed the walls on a sunny day, brightening the room that hitherto had been a kind of empty store, quite literally a cold space. Now the little, recessed window, shining in white gloss, was to become the child's first lookout to the glowing dawns of that summer. It was all going to be so different.

The house was not the only place to be readied. For, although no infant would notice, and only six months previously I might have thought the idea absurd, now for this baby that was somewhere out there, the farm and garden also had to be prepared. No animal was to be sick. No weeds were to be rioting inwards over the potato ridges. Everything must be in its proper place, set, newly in order.

Chris woke in the mornings and hurried to it. Into the slow peace of our days had come a new purpose that informed every living thing. After two growing seasons, Chris had mastered the main garden. She had begun to know it like a friend, or an enemy. She knew what could and couldn't survive here. She poured her energy into the making of the varied palette of a new flower garden. These would be flowers of celebration.

I watched from the writing table or joined her at the work, and it seemed to me that in the simplicity of resurrecting and remaking this garden lay a kind of personal history of our lives here. It was something all gardeners know. The way seasons dated things, the way you looked out at each year's new blossom and thought: we put the peonies in our first year here and never thought they would last. There is the Centaurea that was given to us by Mary and has since taken and spread like crazy. There's last year's new rose, and the pink tulips, and the Siberian wallflowers.

During those warm days in Kiltumper waiting for a baby, we worked new bloom into the garden and imagined next year's flowers seen through a child's eyes.

It's been a long time since I held a baby in my arms. During the long interview process that preceded our being accepted as adoptive parents nobody ever asked me if I knew how to care for a baby. Is it something all mothers know intuitively? In *getting* a baby this way, we are missing out on the natural learning process that seems to accompany the actual carrying of babies for nine months. What do they eat? What do they wear? And in this part of the world, where disposable diapers are a statement of wealth, how do you put a *real* diaper on, as a square or a triangle? You'd think that I'd remember something, being the eldest of six children. But today I am frightened.

Brid Cotter, one of the Cotter family from down the road, herself now a young mother and a trained midwife living in Scotland, called to visit yesterday. She has a two-year-old daughter, and it was easy for her to see my anxiety. Did I know how to bathe a baby, she asked. At first it didn't occur to me that there was anything to it, but as I thought about it I realized that there must be more than just plopping one in the tub. After all, the baby we might be getting would be ten weeks old and not exactly fit for plopping.

Today, Brid arrived at the door with a borrowed baby's tub from Tessie and a naked eighteen-inch rubber doll. Together, we bathed the doll, which didn't squiggle and squirm, I was reminded, and wrapped her up and dressed her in a "nappy."

This is my only initiation so far and I am very grateful for it.

Visitors. Simultaneously, two of our good friends from America, Cyndi and Matt, and Chris's brother Sean arrived for a stay, and we were delighted to have a full house for the first time this year. For us, of course, visitors in summertime mean help on the farm. Since the episode with Gerty, the cows and calves had remained quietly in Tumper, a pastoral picture of perfect harmony. It was in the spongy vastness of the bog that we needed help and all visitors were "invited" to join us there.

There is something about Kiltumper, a timeless appeal. Chris and I were not the only ones who were measuring the quality of our lives here. Set apart and cut off from the myriad distractions of life in Manhattan, days and nights in Kiltumper are perfect countryside settings for the quiet contemplation of a career, a love, a life. In this green isolation, whole chunks of life can suddenly seem unimportant. A walk across fields in the evening light can change philosophies forever. It was the spirit of the place, the same spirit that would make Sean cancel his plans in New York and extend his time with us to rehang the gate into Tumper, remake a fallen drain, and cut and split the timber of three ash trees for our winter fuel. It was the same spirit that informed evenings by the fire. At first Cyndi, Matt, and Sean had sat in the kitchen after dinner with the expectant look of people ready to go somewhere. But there are no movies to go to, much less restaurants or clubs.

"Of course, nightlife here means something else entirely," I said.

"What's that, Niall?" asked Matt, leaning forward on his chair, as if expecting to hear of some dramatic, highly secret Irish entertainment. Upon his lap I saw a copy of W. B. Yeats's *Folk and Fairy Tales of Ireland.*

"Nightlife," I said, "is spiritlife, the spirits coming out of the fairy-forts."

"The what?"

"The fairy-forts," I said. "Don't tell me you haven't heard of fairy-forts? Chris, can you believe this? They haven't heard of the fairy-forts!"

There was a pause, then there was a chorus of cynical New York reaction. I had been reading earlier that day about the power of stories in old Ireland before the influx of television and cinema. All the *seanachais*, the storytellers, are almost gone now from the West, but the ability to tell a good tale is still something held in admiration and respect. It wasn't of the quaintness of fairytales that I wanted to speak. It wasn't to make the country seem any more charming, but rather to try and test out the credibility that imaginary things can have when told at nighttime before the open hearth fire. I wanted to see if words could work a little magic. Even on three New Yorkers.

"Sure, Niall," said Sean, "Fairy-forts! Come on!"

"Listen." I dropped my voice to a serious and urgent whisper. "I don't care if you believe me or not, but fairy-forts exist." I paused and gazed into the fire. "There's one on this farm."

"Where?" It was Matt's voice.

"In the Fort Field," I said, "down by Downeses'."

"It is, Sean," said Chris. "It's there. You can see it from the road."

"Sure, Chris. Sure. This is only put on for the Yanks, I know."

"Is it really called the Fort Field?" asked Cyndi. "How come we haven't gone down to see it?"

With that I knew that here was an opportunity for fun. "Let me tell you a few things about fairy-forts," I said, "before you want to go tramping around one. Fairy-forts are highly superstitious places. Now, for example, Chris and I have heard several true stories since we came here, and honestly, they would frighten you with what has happened to people. . ." And so began that evening's quiet fireside telling of fairy stories. We had heard them told by better storytellers than ourselves, and in the retelling they were remixed and reshaped to suit the night, and yet still they held a strangely real power. With Chris's help and asides, assuring Matt, Sean, and Cyndi that "this one is definitely true," I told of a man, Pat O'Mahon, who had a passionate love for dancing. "Every night Pat would be out in the village dancing until the pubs closed and he was sent walking home along the road. He was at this for several years and was known all around the parish as a man mad for dancing. Well then, one night he was coming home from Kilmihil and he saw a bunch of fairies dancing inside in their fairy-fort. "Come in and dance a Clare set for us, Pat," one of the fairies called out to him, and with that of course he climbed up on the ditch and across into the field. Without further delay, the finest dancing music he ever heard in his life started up. He couldn't make out where the music was coming from exactly, but he threw down his cap, took the arm of one of the fairies next to him and started dancing away like mad."

I paused for a moment; they were listening.

"Well now, Pat O'Mahon danced that night until morning when suddenly, without exactly knowing how, he found himself back out on the road walking home. The sweetness of the music was still playing in his head, and yet he only had the dimmest recollection of where he had been and what had happened to him. He arrived home to his wife and sat down in the kitchen trying to figure it out. "Where'd you leave your cap?" she asked him. And of course that was it. He reached up to the top of his head—no cap. And then he remembered. "I've been away dancing with the fairies," he said. Of course the wife burst out laughing. She was a big, kind woman. Her sister is still living down in the village. But anyway, a terrible sadness came over Pat then and he resolved that he would never go out dancing again because never again would he hear as sweet a music as he had heard with the fairies. From that day he took to his bed and wouldn't rise. Everyone in the village was talking about it, the spell that had been cast on Pat O'Mahon the night he entered the fairy-fort. The priest came up to try and get him out of it, but no, Pat was going to stay in that bed until the day he died.

"Well, years passed. Pat became an old man. And then, one midsummer's morning, the wife heard him stirring inside in the bedroom. Out on his weak, bandy legs he came, into the light of the kitchen for the first time in years. "What are you doing?" she marveled to him, as he looked around at the new wallpaper, the chairs, the way she had changed things over the years. "I'm going dancing," he announced, almost falling over he was so unused to standing.

"Well that day, noon, and night, Pat O'Mahon went dancing. He was wild for it. And to those who saw him—and some of the people in the village still remember—they said he had a kind of distant happy look on his face all the time, dancing even when there was no music playing. He danced home that night, danced in the door in the moonlight, and the first thing the wife noticed was the old cap on his head. Well, that night he went to bed, dancing even in his sleep, dancing, dancing, dancing until the very moment of dawn when the silent music seemed to stop, and all at once as if the strings on a puppet were cut, Pat O'Mahon dropped dead."

I finished in a whisper and rose to put turf on the fire. It was working, the spell of the thing was in the room even after the story ended. For a moment there was an absolute hush. "Well, I'm going to bed," I said and crossed to the bathroom. I will give them three minutes, I thought.

In three minutes I came out into the kitchen.

"Niall," said Sean, "will you take us down to the fairy-fort?"

"When?"

"Now. We want to go down to see it now."

"I wouldn't go down there at night. Would you, Chris?"

"No, never," she said.

We let it play like this for another few moments, watching the draw of a fairy story work upon our spellbound visitors. Then, feigning reluctance, I pulled on my coat and led Sean, Matt, and Cyndi out the back door. It was pitch dark. Past midnight and moonless, the night enveloped us in blackness. Without light anywhere and walking huddled together on a muddied, potholed road, the three doubters clung to each other's coats and called out to me if I led too many steps ahead of them. In the absolute darkness, of course, imaginations ran wild. By the time we had reached the Fort Field echoes of fairies and the strains of fabulous night music were everywhere. We crossed into the field in a tight little bunch, seeing no further than ten feet in front of us. The fort, a raised circular mound crowned by a weirdly bent whitethorn tree, was all in shadows. "Is this it?" asked Cyndi in a reverential whisper. "I'm not coming in, but you have a very nice house," she said. From behind me somewhere I could hear Matt quietly murmuring: "Nice fairies, nice fairies. . ."

It was at that moment I thought I heard something moving in the field. Or at least that's what I said, sharply whispering, "Wait! Stay here, don't move!" and stepped quickly away from the fort where our three visitors were huddled in the darkness. From the side of the ditch, unseen, I peered back.

"Niall? Niall, where are you?" I heard their calls turn urgent. "Niall, this isn't funny, you know, get back here now!" And then I saw their blurry night shapes gradually begin to stumble about in the dark field. They knew it was a joke, or did they? I wondered, watching as they clung to each other's coats and inched timidly through the gloom. Perhaps for just a moment they imagined that something had happened to me and I was off with the fairies. I chuckled.

Here was the power of a story. Here was nightlife, I thought, Kiltumper-style.

News at last! Helen called today. Elizabeth seems ready to decide; it looks like she wants *us* to adopt Deirdre!! In fact, if all goes well, we might have her in ten days! Helen told us that it wasn't completely decided yet but very likely. Start getting ready, she said.

The long wait for a baby might be over and yet it's happening faster than anyone imagined. We had expected to wait until Christmas, but now *she's* just around the corner. The wait has tempered our longing with patience. And yet, during this next week while we wait for Helen's final call to say yes, come and get her, or, sorry, not this time, how will we be patient? We must try not to hope too much but, practically speaking, we *have* to get equipped. We have nothing for her but a salmon-colored room with painted white accents and some children's books.

Will we be bringing a baby girl home to Kiltumper Cottage in ten days? How can the preparation time of a full pregnancy squeeze into ten days? We are wildly anxious. What do we need? Everything! Where are the baby showers? Pauline was admiring the baby's room the other day when she remarked as she peered in at the big empty space, "It's beautiful, Crissie, but what's she going to sleep *in?*"

What would she sleep in, what would she eat, what would she wear? "Do you have nappies bought?" Lucy asked me yesterday.

"Nappies? Oh, you mean, diapers . . ." I said.

"Diapers! Good Lord! Here—I got you these to start you off," she said. And from the press she brought a neatly folded stack of twelve of the whitest, softest terry-cloth cotton nappies. So much for disposables! Maybe I'll start a diaper service.

With my mother and my sister so far away in New York, Lucy, Tessie, Mary, and Pauline are advising and helping with everything. They are my constant allies when I feel weak-hearted or overwhelmed, or simply terrified at the idea of a crying child in my arms. Lucy said it would be all right in the end. "Once you have that child in your arms, *you'll* know what to do." And Tessie, already the mother of two beautiful adopted girls, is my steady soul-mate during these short days of my nonpregnancy.

Yesterday, a package arrived for me from my mother. She sent me a large bottle of my favorite perfume, Poison, and reminded me that I'm just as special as any other expectant mother. Thanks, Mom. And today, Niall came home with a bunch of irises from Kilrush. Did I have a craving for anything, he wondered?

Yes, I said, a hot dog!

CHAPTER FOUR

That morning, we woke early from fitful sleeps. I had lit a huge fire in the Stanley range, enough to heat the water and warm the radiator in the baby's room. Chris hurriedly swept corners, hunting out any overlooked cobwebs and washed the breakfast dishes. Dressed in our best clothes, we took a last look at the cottage and closed the door, leaving Kiltumper for the last time as a childless couple. We were on our way, driving to Ennis with one intent: to return with a baby girl. It was a mild Tuesday, the last day in the month of June. In the backseat of the cleaned-out old Peugeot lay an empty carry-cot borrowed from Tessie and some baby blankets, and as we sped along in a kind of silent, entranced dream state, a glance in the rearview mirror kept reminding us it was really happening, after all this time.

We hardly spoke at all, we both had such a strong sense that she was there, somewhere ahead of us, a little girl, ten weeks old. She was an April baby, born on April 16, four days later than Chris's birthdate. Already we knew she was destined for us. She was drawing us nearer to her every moment. When Chris spoke it was with a tight, quivering voice full of emotion.

"I think she was always meant for us, Niall." Chris said. "Sometimes, there are no coincidences. I knew all along that her name would be Deirdre. Deirdre May Williams."

Driving down the narrow little streets of Ennis, it seemed to us as if everyone knew why we were there. I parked the car on O'Connell Street by the lane down to St. Catherine's, and for a moment we sat there, terrified. Should we bring the empty carry-cot in with us? I wondered. It might be unlucky, I decided finally. Instead I grasped Chris's hand and hurried down the lane.

We were met by a woman at the reception desk who led us up two flights of banistered stairs to the large, pale room on the second floor that had already become familiar to us. It was here, many months before, that the whole process had begun. Now tables and chairs were all neatly stacked away in a corner and the floor was empty. Opening the door, the woman smiled at us and went back downstairs: Helen would be along in a minute.

The buzz of the busy streets of Ennis suddenly receded. In the vast room we felt like small souls as we huddled by the window in a tiny ray of sunlight.

"What's going to happen?" asked Chris. "Will Helen just walk in with the baby?"

"I don't know."

"God. What if she looks at us and starts crying."

"She won't, Chris."

"She won't have any idea of who we are."

Helen opened the door. She had no baby in her arms.

"So, how are you?" she said, with a great smile, crossing to the window to take a warm hold of our hands.

"Terrified," I said.

"Why, Niall? Are you terrified too, Chris?" she asked. "You've nothing to be afraid of. She's a lovely little baby."

Chris let out a little cry. "Where is Deirdre now?" she asked anxiously.

"She's downstairs asleep. Will I get her?"

We nodded.

Helen left us. Baby Deirdre was suddenly going to appear, to come into our lives the very moment that door re-opened. It was a moment that stretched out to encompass every day of our six-year marriage, our two years of waiting. We heard and said nothing. I grasped Chris's hand. When Helen appeared in the doorway with a little yellow bundle in her arms, I felt our fingers tighten.

There she was, Baby Deirdre.

"Well, which of you is going to take her from me?" The two of us stood there frozen to the spot. Chris looked at me and I held out my arms.

For the rest of the hour that we spent there in that room with Deirdre, so much that happened seemed to take place in a kind of incredible dreamlike haze. Vaguely, I remember, Helen left us for a few moments. We passed the sleeping baby between us and hugged her tightly, smelling the sweet infant smell of her that seemed so warm and clean and new. That smell stays with me more than anything. I find it whenever I think of her then, that extraordinary breath of purity, the sheer loveliness of holding her close and feeling life. When she awoke she cried, and Helen quickly came back into the room with Father Geoghegan, the president of the society. They stood beside us as we desperately tried to quieten Deirdre. She stopped for a moment, looked at us, seemed to giggle, and then cried again. When she cried, our hearts went out to her in such a wrenching, deep-felt way that it seemed almost a pain of our own. Chris took her from me and the room suddenly hushed.

There were things spoken to us by Helen, by Father Geoghegan, but we barely heard them. She was ours. For the moment, anyway. She was ten weeks old and had fair skin and blue, blue eyes. I slipped outside to get the carry-cot.

In a trance I unlocked the car and brought out the empty carry-cot. People passing seemed to glance curiously at me, and I felt awkward and embarrassed hurrying up the crowded street with it. A light rain was starting to fall as the bells of the cathedral chimed the noon hour.

Upstairs, Deirdre was asleep in Chris's arms. Helen went over our final instructions; she would telephone that evening to see how we were managing, she'd call at the house in a day or two.

"Here are the foster mother's instructions on Deirdre's sleeping and eating patterns. Okay? Is that all right?" She handed us a small blue envelope.

And with that, and handshakes from Father Geoghegan and kisses from Helen, we left. I lifted the carry-cot with Deirdre inside it for the first time and with Chris beside me walked very carefully down the two flights of stairs, suddenly conscious of every tiny thing that might harm or trouble her. We opened the front door to the noise of midday and felt the coolness of the air as if we were newborn ourselves. Was she wrapped warmly enough? Delicately maneuvering out into the street, I watched her minute sleeping expressions as a beam of stray sunlight fell across her face. Was she happy or sad? Was that a smile she made in a dream?

Sitting in the car and realizing that we were, right then, actually going to bring home a real baby, we both felt like shouting but said nothing for fear of waking her. We were past Lissycasey and more than halfway home before Chris took out the foster mother's instructions. On a small lined piece of blue paper were handwritten notes under the heading BABY DEIRDRE:

"Baby Deirdre is on four to five feeds a day. She takes a full bottle of milk at each feed. Sometimes she may need more milk. Baby Deirdre is on iron drops at the moment. She has a rash on the nappy area.

"Deirdre sleeps in a cot in her own room. She goes to bed at ten o'clock at night. Deirdre has a feed during the night. Baby Deirdre gets cross at times. She goes for a walk every day in the pram. Baby Deirdre has a nap in the morning around nine o'clock."

Chris finished reading out the note and looked over at me. One phrase had struck both of us at the same time, and as we turned off the main road, past Knockalough lake into Kilmihil, Chris read it out again. "Baby Deirdre gets cross at times." What could it mean? Visions of a bawling child roaring in the kitchen raced before us. We drove on home not a little terrified of the sleeping infant in the backseat.

Deirdre's first night with us. And we had visitors galore. All well-wishers. Tessie and Lucy came to lend a hand and to see how the nervous new parents were getting on. They came with cards and gifts. Pauline came up with two little yellow Babygro's. Mary and Breda came with cards, a five-pound note in each. At one point, there were five kind friends sitting on our one couch offering encouraging words as I lifted Deirdre into her little bathtub and began to bathe her. I was a nervous wreck, sure that I was doing it wrong. I was awkward at it, but nobody said so. They said it was good to bathe her. In fact, if there is one remark that everyone seems to share it's this: Bathe her once a day. They said it'll tire her out and she'll sleep well. And thank God, she loves it. She never cries. I dressed her slowly, fumbling and afraid that her little head would fall off if I bumped it. Then, I gave her a bottle, burping her every two ounces to a chorus of motherly coos from my friends. At midnight we put her into her carry-cot. We expected to have to wake at four to feed her again. I was still waiting for Deirdre to get cross. But she went straight to sleep. We went to bed in expectation of waking at four for a hungry, cross baby. I lay there, waiting and waiting, wondering if she was still breathing. She was in the kitchen right next to us and I could hear every sleeping gurgle that she made. But she kept sleeping. The little angel didn't wake at four, at five, at six, or at seven, but stirred with the rest of the world at the very proper hour of eight! Who was that cross baby?

Suddenly life in the cottage was made up of diapers and safety pins and bottles of milk, as well as laughter, of advice from all quarters, of amazement at every gesture, movement, expression, of telling everyone when they asked that "yes, she slept through all of last night again," of shaking a single rattle doll for minutes on end, of propping her up and picking her up and putting her down, of simply being there, the three of us in the kitchen watching clouds scud on a blue sky. So far it was easy. And the little, "cross" baby with the terrible nappy rash and cradle cap was nothing but a wonder. Of course, she did immediately change the shape of our days in Kiltumper. We were no longer both as free to devote our time to the typewriter, the garden, or the farm as we had been over the course of the previous two years. And yet, we had in many ways a unique situation. Although we wanted to follow what Chris called traditional methods, starting the baby on a tight routine for feeding and sleeping, and sticking to it, we were both working at home together, and in this closeness hoped to share as much as possible in caring for Deirdre. Simply put, I wanted to be around her as much as Chris was. And yet we both wanted our work to go on, too. We knew that time spent outside was equally important for each of us, whether in the garden, at the weeds, or at the easel, or simply out on the bog or the fields. In the first weeks of our new parenthood then, we talked schedules and made plans. Insofar as possible, I would take the morning shift, Chris the afternoons. Among the items of our borrowed baby gear (how quickly the cottage was full of it!)—a carry-cot and crib from Tessie, a baby bath from Maura Cotter, a baby "bouncer" and wicker bassinet from Evelyn Johnston, baby blankets and a baby pillow from Lucy, clothes, and toys from everybody.

Deirdre had been given a marvelous new playpen by Polly, Chris's stepmother. Every time Deirdre was fed and changed she lay in it in a kind of curious contentment watching her world go by. A small blue Snugli had come from Danna, Chris's sister-in-law in California, and in the days and weeks ahead Chris or I would strap it on and take it out where it had never dreamed it would be, on the hill fields of west Clare, moving through our little herd of animals with Deirdre snuggled inside it.

With the sudden arrival of warm sunny weather, the

countryside about us buzzed with activity, and tractors sputtered through the mornings. Now hay was the business of the day and as cows grazed and lay out lazily on warm grassy slopes, our neighbors worked from morning until night harvesting winter fodder. Our own farm needed tending. Wading out into the middle of the five acres of wild flowers and buttercups that were the Big Meadow in July, Michael told me the hay could wait for another ten days. We would gamble on dry weather holding, or coming again then. In the meantime, the bog beckoned.

This year, our third time cutting turf from the bog on Tumper, we had been late with everything. I had only gone to it for the first time in late May: three breezy halfdays when Martin and Brendan, young men from the village, had joined me on the brown bogland that sits about a mile up from the cottage. Sharing the cutting of the turf, they had watched my comical haste as I tried to run Paddy Cotter's turf barrow with the punctured bicycle wheel across the heathery land to unload. *Pisogs*, or little tufts of grass, were enough to unbalance the barrow, and more often than not it toppled before I meant it to. It was hard work, but good work. In two years we had come to know the crucial business of saving turf in the bog of Kiltumper quite well. We knew the labor of cutting days as each "bar," or layer, of turf was cut out of the ground by the *sleadoir*, or slanesman, with the winged spade, or *slan*. We knew the way steps were carved out of the turf itself as each layer brought the turf cutter further downward into the soft squelchy underbelly of the bog where the fuel was best. We knew the right-handed glove worn to help prevent blistering of the palm from the unusual down and up right-to-left motion of the cutting and laying out of each sod on the bank. We knew the switch from boots to Wellingtons as the turf cutter found himself six feet down in bogwater and black turf. By now, we knew the very nature of our bank. We knew the soft places which the barrow wheel would cut up with the constant crossing of bringing the turf away twenty yards to unload. We knew the best places to scatter the sods to catch every air of every breeze and stroke of sunlight for the important business of drying. We had become intimate with the place. In May, with Martin and Brendan, we had cut what I had hoped was more than enough turf to warm the cottage for the winter. I had been thinking there might be three of us, and with that thought stood back to look over the scattered new- cut sods gleaming in the light. Laid out end to end up there, they covered a space forty yards by twenty. But after two wet summers when each of a thousand pieces of turf had had to be handled seven or eight times, turning them over and over in the air in an effort to dry them slowly, I had wondered: would this year be any different? Cutting turf late into the first week of June, were we already too late?

Weather, of course, is everything here. By July, the turf was still far from "won" home, but as the long days of bright summer suddenly came dazzling over the fields, hope touched everything. These were the days to second "foot," or stack, the turf. With Martin and Brendan's help, it had already been footed once, each sod stood on end in little groups of four or five with a top-sod on balance. The stacks, or *grogans*, would be partially dry, but in order to catch every natural power of drying in the wind and sun, the little *grogans* had to be remade.

Early in the morning I left Chris with Deirdre in the cottage and walked through the cows, up the back hill to do the work. The haymakers were already moving into their meadows, and from the top of the hill, looking away out to the south and the sun-hazy mountains of Kerry, the stone-walled patterns of green and gold marked the landscape like a tapestry of labor. Here and there cut meadows were dotted with new trams, or haystacks, and in the marvelous silence of the distance tiny tractors seemed to move effortlessly cutting hay in great yellowing circular patterns as round and round a field the mower went like a clockwork toy. Nearer to us, I could see the farms of our neighbors. Michael was cutting the fields below our cottage today. Sean had two meadows of hay down. Michael Dooley and Michael Donnellan had been out in the meadows for an hour already. For the next month or so they would all be at it in one way or another, cutting, turning, second turning, baling or tramming hay. The women would be drawn into it, too, and every evening would be a tired one while the weather held. Going up into the bog that morning I wished we were at our own hay and felt a foreboding sense that the summer wouldn't hold. But before the thought of hungry cows came the picture of my new daughter in the cold house in December and January. Turf, Chris had said, go up to the turf. She said it holding the happy baby in a beam of warm light by the kitchen window.

It was with the energy of urgency then that I took off my sweater in the sunshine and bent down to begin refooting the turf on the bog. I was alone up there as I had been many times before. And yet there was a different feeling to the work. Not only did I feel the sensation of all the labor in bog and meadow that was going on ceaselessly about me, but more than that, I felt part of something larger. I worked on with incredible gladness there and handled the sods like pieces of the day itself. Windless time passed and the warm light of July bathed the bog with sunshine. The first sharp dried edges of the turf almost broke off in my hands and I felt a wave of faith sweep across the purple and green of heather and moss: this turf would fully dry, I heard myself say. This summer would be good.

For the rest of the morning that same lightness and hope filled every moment of my working. There, on the bog of Kiltumper, I felt giddily happier than I had ever felt before. I worked steadily, bending and unbending to the turf in a kind of mesmeric serenity, when suddenly it came to me: everything was being made new, I thought. I am seeing and feeling everything newly now. In this work is the child. I am a father now.

Thank God for this warm weather. I actually had to go to Ennis today specifically to get Deirdre a sun hat! It's sizes too large for her but she looks fantastic. The sun is too strong for her eyes, but she likes to be outside. So on these lovely sunny afternoons I prop her up in the carry-cot and affix an umbrella to it. I *know* it's good for her to be outside. We've talked to Dr. Harty, the young family doctor who lives in Kilmihil with his beautiful wife and their three children, and he is guiding us on matters of immunization and feeding. We know many parents start their babies on solid food earlier than six months, but as Deirdre is very happy on the bottle formula for hungry babies that she gets, we're following Dr. Harty's advice and only feeding Deirdre four eight-ounce bottles a day. We will hold off giving her solids until she's about six months. Having never raised a baby before we're depending upon our own good sense. The nearest pediatrician is in Limerick, an hour's drive from here, where we hope never to have to call him. As for what we can't get here, compared to the plethora of baby products in the United States, who knows? All I can say is that Deirdre is happy and healthy and thriving "west Clare" style.

Yesterday, I took her over to the hens' cabin so she could see them moving about and pecking the grass. We've had those hens for over two years and as they didn't seem to be laying with any regularity, I offered them to Breda for Michael's greyhounds. Sounds cruel, I know, but it is costly to feed them just for the fun of it. I'll ask Annette O'Leary for some new young hens, or pullets. Fairly soon, Deirdre should be getting a fresh yolk, so they say around here, and the pullets might be laying by autumn. We waved good-bye to the hens as Niall gathered them and put them in an old feed bag. Wherefore go our hens? I better not tell her, exactly. Bye bye, hens. Say "bye bye," Deirdre.

Changes. Yesterday I read in the paper that all over the west of Ireland the traditional cottages are rapidly disappearing to be replaced, for the most part, by modern single-story houses, or bungalows. The very face of the West is changing, reports the journalist, decrying the loss of yet another part of old Ireland and laying the blame squarely at the feet of those who live in some of the most scenic parts of the country.

All day after reading this I was troubled and went about the business of the farm turning the question over in my mind. On the one hand, like everyone else who witnesses the passing of the thatched cottage, we have felt the sadness of seeing roofs rot and fall in on dwellings that have become nothing more than cow shelters in spectacular settings along the Atlantic coastline. Old ways *are* dying out, and the thatchers are all gone, nearly. The image of the man in a white shirt upon the summer roof, with hazel rods and knives working all day to remake the house for the winter is quickly fading into the past. And yet, with him, fading too are the cottage's cross-drafts from window and half-door, the seat by the fire with half the body warmed and the other half freezing, the rheumatic chills, the going out for water in all sorts of weather, the down-puffs of turf smoke, the soot falls and hailstones in the kitchen, the little brownish light the tiny windows let in, a litany of complaints. All these comfortless parts of cottage life are already passing into folk memory, regretted more by the sightseers than by the cottage dwellers, yet not entirely unmourned even by them.

In our way, we, too, had brought change to Kiltumper. Since the day we first entered the cottage, an accommodation had begun, a gradual matching of person and place. And although we both felt strongly that we wanted to retain all we could of the look and feel of the place, now with Deirdre in the back room the urgency of keeping the house warm and dry overtook our misgivings about bringing about more change. Already we had gone through each of the rooms trying to close down drafts. Up in the dust of the garret room, we had found an old brownish photograph of Chris's grandfather's family. The prodigal son who had done well in America had sent back a family portrait to be shown around the hearth whenever neighbors came visiting on the *cuaird*. We had hung that photograph by the kitchen window with another like it of the O'Connell family in 1914 (from Chris's mother's side). Two sepia-toned portraits of Irish families in America overlooked the slow changes we were bringing to this cottage in Clare—the place the Breens had left behind.

During July, with two large rolls of stuff brought from Kilrush, I climbed up inside the small space between the old ceilings of the house and the roof. The great pitch-blackened joists, the unplastered stones of the walls here and there tilted off plumb, the little wedges of wood or paper stuck in their crevices, untouched for ages, were disclosed to me. I saw the house from a new vantage point. Dry, powdery dustiness coated the stones, and cobwebs draped corners thick as netting. The age and character of the building, seen from high inside it, gave me a slight sense of unease. For we were going to change it; this seemed inevitable. A new room would be warmer for the baby; when the cold damp days of winter came it would hold the heat and banish to memory those comically frosty mornings of our first winter in Kiltumper when our noses and ears froze in the bed and we had to wear gloves to read a book at bedtime.

We would all be more comfortable. And yet, we felt at times almost as if we had betrayed something. It was a feeling all tangled up with the worst kind of nostalgia, a romanticism that ignored such nuisances as drafts and leaks, spiders and mice. And still it was there, a whispered query from every one of the old people who had ever lived here wintering by the hearth without bathroom or water. Were we not as hardy as they? We were not. We had to overcome that soft lulling force that wanted always to keep things as they were. It was something to be reckoned with. We had come here two years ago, I would argue with myself, as I layed out the insulation, not to recreate the nineteenth century, not to do without water or light, but to seek a way of life, for the time being, that included peace-fulness and quiet, a sense of slowness and time, in an old country growing older in the rain. We had come to write and to paint. And now, to raise a child. Perhaps, all along, that is why we're here.

Above the ceiling, up inside the dusty head of the house, I tried to reason it out with the voice of the ancestors, the ghosts of Kiltumper: through Deirdre new life would come to these rooms and spaces. Everything old was being renewed. For the first time in half a century these thick stone walls would shelter a child.

With money from Chris's father and a grant from the government for the improvement of pre-1920 houses, we set about adding a new bedroom to the house. We would build it above the kitchen; the heat of the range, rising, would make it our warmest room. During the days of summer, we watched anxiously as a local builder and his sons dropped the kitchen ceiling and, carefully removing the slates, opened the house to the elements. Unroofed and open, with sweeps of white cloud passing slowly over it, the place seemed oddly fragile. Daylight fell where no light had fallen, dust and cobwebs looked silvery in the sunshine, and for days wheelbarrows of stuff, stones and timbers, were carted out like so much guts. Then, as the walls of the new room rose at the back of the building, it began to seem as if our dwelling here had brought a tangible new vigor to the house.

But the day after the room was finished, Chris and I stood upstairs looking in dismay down the steep garret stair to the kitchen below. A fine bedroom had been added to the house; it was bright and spacious. There was only one problem: in the decision to keep the changes to a minimum and retain the old stair something had been overlooked. The steps, rising as they always had at a sharp angle into the new, lowered kitchen ceiling, passed through an opening that was less than four feet wide.

The bed, the famous white ash bed that had been our first piece of furniture in the house, and for which we had waited so long, would not, could not fit upstairs! Dismantled to its smallest, it was still too large. No matter who came to the house to look at it, Michael, Mary, Larry, or Lucy, none of them could see how we could get the bed upstairs. We had a warm bedroom, but without a bed.

For ten days the weather held. In brilliant sunlight I worked with a fork in Michael's meadows across the road, watched the skies, and worried about our own hay. It was nearly ready to cut. Each morning I went out into the back field to try and gauge the growth, walking out into the ripe center of the golden grasses and wild flowers. I stood there, knee-high in mid-field, and looked at all the cut meadows about me. Haystacks stood gaily dotted about in everyone else's fields. But still our haybarn was empty. Chris and I grew more nervous every day now. There was something calm and trusting about the farmers around us that we didn't have yet. We still looked at the rhythm of the farm year much as we used to look at work deadlines and schedules in our offices in Manhattan: cows calving in April, grazing in Upper and Lower Tumper May and June, saving hay first week of July. We weren't yet used to being farmers, nor had we fully learned the lesson that had been taught to us over and over since we first arrived in Clare: the perception of time is entirely different here. Things happen when they're ready to happen, and not before. I stepped my way back out of the meadow carefully that morning walking backwards in the places where my feet had already flattened flowers. And an hour later I heard the tractor coming to cut our hay.

Wherefore go our hens I had wondered when Deirdre and I waved good-bye to them. Well, funny thing. They're alive and doing well. Martin Keane stopped by last evening and on his way out said, "Your hens are doing well, you'll be happy to hear." "How do you know?" I asked, quite curious at this news of my resurrected hens. "Well, two of them are over at my house." "Are they laying?" I asked him. "They are," he replied and I was pleased to hear it. Meanwhile I pieced together the journey of my three hens. When they got to Breda's, it turned out that Michael didn't need them for the greyhounds. So, they traveled further afield to Keanes', who have a menagerie of domestic and farmyard animals, and while waiting a day or two in the cabin before being slaughtered suddenly started laying. Reprieved, it seems they're all happy as Larry there!

Ribs of hay traveled the field on a slow-motion breeze. The air glistened. Blackbirds swooped down and rose before the mower and frogs leapt from underfoot. Within half an hour the meadow was "down" and great concentric circles of loose hay lay all around the field. Every moment of sunlight, every breath of every dry breeze counted. We needed two days of good weather. In two days the hay would be turned by machine three or four times, each time growing lighter as every drop of moisture was dried from it. Then it would be baled and brought to the hay-barn. A single shower of rain would set the whole process back to the beginning. A day's heavy rain could ruin the harvest altogether.

If time had seemed to stretch lazily on forever before, now it was tightly concentrated into two orbits of the sun. These were the two single most important days of our farming year, and meant the difference between good and bad winter fodder for our cows.

With Deirdre in her arms, Chris walked out into the evening meadow.

"I think it's going to rain, Niall," she said.

"No, it's not. It hasn't rained for ten days."

"I know, that's what I'm afraid of. What do you think, Deirdre, is it going to rain?" She held the baby high up in the sunset air. From deep in her throat Deirdre let out a great giggle.

"You see," I said, "not a chance of rain!"

That night, however, with the hay lying in the back meadow, I slept as poorly as I have ever slept and woke often imagining I heard the first spatterings of morning rain.

As the early dew dried off the following morning, clear blue skies stretched away to the west as far as the eye could see. After walking out into the middle of the meadow I went in to have breakfast and wait. After an hour I began to wonder: surely it was time now to start turning it again? Again, with the impatience of city people we grew frantic with the passing of every half hour. Then, in a kind of well-intentioned act of assertion, I took our one hayfork and walked out into the five-acre field to toss and turn the hay by hand. Almost at once I heard a tractor coming up the road and had to hurry to hide the evidence of my foolishness as another of our neighbors, Paul O'Shea, drove up, singing country music tunes to himself as he sped off around the meadow turning the hay into the air like crazy. It seemed everyone knew when hay was down, and there was an unspoken pact between people along a road that sent help when help was needed. Michael was gone to someone else's meadow; he'd be back to me later, back to them later still, until the last sounds of the tractors would die off into the gloaming. Harvest time is a time Chris and I have come to love here, for it is during haymaking that the marvelous generosity and the bond of community feeling of old Ireland lives on.

Haying makes for a long day. Everyone is part of it. The women make huge stacks of thickly buttered ham or cheese sandwiches for the workers and cut great big wedges of fresh brownbread. Flasks and milk bottles of tea are brought into the meadows and for a little time men sit at the butt of a tram and the work stops. Hayforks stand at angles in the ground. Then it's back to the work. In the afternoon young children bring bottles of water from the house, and return with refills. The women come out and join in, tying cords over the top of the trams, following a little behind the men as the meadow is saved and the haystacks counted. There is nothing like it. There's a feeling in the air you can almost touch; it's like faith rewarded, the land giving returns for cold wet Spring days, sodden fields, and muck everywhere.

When the hay in our back meadow had been turned that morning Paul stopped the tractor over by the wall and leaped down. He was wearing a red baseball cap that he pushed back on his head as he picked up a handful of hay. He sang the last words of his song as he looked at it.

"That's lovely hay there, Niall," he said.

"Is it?" I said.

"Oh gosh yes. Lovely hay."

"When do you think I'll be able to bale it, Paul? "

"Are you going baling it or tramming it?"

"Baling, if it's dry enough."

"That's it, if it's dry enough. Well sure, I suppose another dry day and you could bale it."

Another dry day. It seemed to be tempting fate. If the hay were baled too soon we knew it would heat and rot in the haybarn. During the two previous wet summers, we had heard stories of whole harvests turning to black, steamy soggy stuff, good for nothing. The drying was everything. There was nothing for it but to go back into the house or out into the garden and try to forget our anxiety about the weather.

After an hour or so a car pulled up at the front gate with engine trouble. I walked out to offer help. Sabra, a good friend—my ex-boss in Manhattan—popped up from the backseat. "Surprise!"

She had arrived in Shannon with her husband David, and come to see for herself just what had become of that quiet clean-shaven copywriter she had once worked so hard.

"You *look* like a farmer, Niall," she said, as I led them into the house. Deirdre was awake and lying quietly in the carry-cot, and so for an hour or two we sat with mugs of tea, discussing babies, cows, gardens, books, and the few people I knew who were still at the office.

"Well, Sabra," I said, after a while, not quite forgetting that I was speaking to my former boss, "you've come at the busiest time of our year. How would you feel about putting on some working clothes and helping us with the hay tomorrow?"

Sabra looked at David, David looked at me. "We'd love to," he said. "We'll be here tomorrow morning around ten."

The following morning I woke to find Michael out in the back meadow before me. We stood there in the perfect stillness of very early morning with the day poised before us and the field full of birds. "See him, Niall," Michael said, pointing up into the field above us where a large hare was scampering homewards through the grass. We watched him a moment, and then Michael turned to walk back to where his tractor was running. "That's lovely hay. It'll be baled today for sure, Niall," he said.

"What time do you think he'll come?" I asked.

"Oh I suppose around lunchtime," he said. "I should be around, I have to go over to Paul's now." And with that he left.

At ten o'clock sharp, Sabra and David arrived, eager for work, and I had to explain that the baler would not be arriving until lunchtime. "What time is that?" said Sabra innocently. "Any time between eleven and three," said Chris.

To entertain our visitors—and not lose the benefit of their marvelous energetic willingness to work—I suggested a trip to the bog. And so, half an hour later, we were crouched on the bog at Tumper second-footing the last of our turf! As images of staff meetings, pink corridors, and sheaves of memoranda rose up against a background of the breezy bogland of west Clare, the incongruity of it brought me near to laughter. Two hours later, as Sabra and David proudly finished the last grogan, my feelings were of admiration. "Fair play to ye," I said, in my best west Clare accent, "but yer great people in the bog!"

Back at the house, after lunch, we waited for the baler to come. The blueness had left the sky and the horizon was a whitish pasty color to the west. Two o'clock: no sign of him. Three o'clock, nothing. I began explaining to our visitors that time in Ireland was an inexact science and to farmers during harvest any time the baler came would be the right time. Chris opened the front door and we sat on in the kitchen, listening for any sound on the road that might indicate that he was coming. This waiting, this interminable suspension between the time appointed and the thing done, was something Chris and I had almost grown to expect since moving back to Ireland. It was by far the hardest thing to adjust to, the lost time, the shop shut for lunch, the town on half-day, the man who said he'd be there, the clockless, unhasty way the whole country tottered forward. Now, here we were in the kitchen, helpers ready, and no sign of the baler. At five o'clock, Sabra and David had to leave for Ennis. Chris grew angry and I walked down the road to see if I could find out where the blazes he was. Francie met me on the road. "He's broken down back at Cree," he said. "Daddy said he'll be here in a while."

In a while. There was nothing left of the blue day now. I looked out at the cut hay and thought I saw the first signs of rain. At seven o'clock that evening another car drove up bringing Martin Murray, Martin Dunne, and Brendan Sheedy. "We've come to put in your bales for you," said Martin cheerfully. We marched into the kitchen. Ten minutes later, Martin Keane arrived. Now we had four helpers and no work. I couldn't stand it. It seemed so stupid, so desperately backward. I couldn't sit still.

"You could tram the hay into small cocks, and when he comes in the morning knock them out for him to bale," Martin Keane suggested. "That way if it rains tonight, it won't do much harm."

In a wave of urgency the four of us went at the hay with two-pronged forks. This very ordinary part of summer was made extraordinary for us. The first trams rose like magic and wisps of golden hay floated on the evening air. Big Martin Murray handled the hayfork like a toy, shouldering great heaps of the stuff up onto a tram and moving on to the next. We had made half a dozen, and then, at long last, we heard the baler arrive. The driver raced off around the meadow, shunting out bales behind him. In forty-five minutes he had done the work that would have taken me days. On towards midnight, in the last of fading light, he sped off down the road to another farmer who was still waiting for him.

For another hour, the three Martins and Brendan helped me bring in the bales. They were stacked in blocks high into the haybarn. A warm jubilant mood of satisfaction rose in each of us despite our exhaustion. A thin drizzle was starting to fall as we went into the house with the last of the hay saved. Great stacks of sandwiches were laid upon the kitchen table. With fresh brownbread, a jam and cream sponge cake, and warm Madeira cake, Chris spread the harvest feast and splashed out the tea.

CHAPTER
FIVE

We had a fine bedroom with no bed in it. For a month or so we tried to figure it out: how were we to manage to get a bed into the bright, warm new room upstairs? In the meantime, we still slept in our cavernous bedroom in the corner of the house, a cold room even in August. Despite all we had done since moving into the house, a heavy dampness often pervaded the rooms away from the main fire. Clothes in the bedroom wardrobe needed continual airing, little bits of green flufflike mold were discovered on woolen jackets. Brown damp stains sullied the white-washed walls. It was the thickness of the walls, we were told, obscurely. It was a leaky roof. The stones weeped. Many explanations were offered, but no remedies. Like-wise, many colorful suggestions and contrary counsels on how to get the bed into the bedroom filled our heads as we lay down to sleep.

"I know," said Chris one evening as we sat in the kitchen and listened to Atlantic breezes rushing through the dark leaves of the ash trees outside. "A futon and a dehumidifier!"

"What?" asked Martin Murray, who was with us on the *cuaird*.

"A futon for upstairs and a dehumidifier to dry out the dampness down here."

"What is a futon, when it's at home?" asked Martin. He was used to Chris's American suggestions, but he still smiled at their seeming oddity.

"A Japanese bed."

"A *Japanese* bed!"

"Yes. They're made of crushed cotton and they roll up," she explained. "I'm sure they have them somewhere in Ireland, probably in Galway. And a dehumidifier is a machine that dries out dampness. Lots of people in America use them, and I'd think that in a place like Ireland they're bound to have them."

A Japanese bed that rolls up and a machine that dries out dampness. In the morning we put Deirdre in the backseat and drove to Ennis on our double quest. The town had come to mean a lot to us. It was the place where we had first seen the prettiest little girl in the world—our daughter. Towns like Ennis are few and far between. The narrow winding streets house a hundred little shops of all kinds and shapes. Some have modern fronts, but many retain the brightly painted old-style wooden shopfront. Sometimes Chris drives into the town just to get a glimpse of a crowd of people doing extravagant things like eating publike food in publike places, or buying "French" baguettes in the many bakeries, or shopping in a supermarket.

In our first two years here we have learned that there is

often more to these western towns and villages than meets the eye, and among the fantastic things some of the old general stores have stocked away, who was to say there mightn't be a dehumidifier? Somehow, however, we doubted that they would have a futon, but we would look.

Driving the old Peugeot that bright August morning, I was reminded of what Thackeray had written about Ennis in his *Irish Sketch Book* of 1842:

"A busy, little, narrow-streeted, foreign-looking town, approached by half-a-mile of thatched cottages, in which I am not ashamed to confess that I saw some as pretty faces as over any half-mile of country I ever travelled in my life . . . At Ennis, as well as everywhere else in Ireland, there were of course the regular number of swaggering-looking buckeens, and shabby-genteel idlers . . . The town was swarming with people; the little dark streets which twist about in all directions being full of cheap merchandise and its vendors. Whether there were many buyers I can't say. I have watched a stall a hundred times in the course of the last three hours and seen no money taken. . ."

The half mile of thatched cottages is gone, the swaggering-looking buckeens and shabby-genteel idlers have been replaced by unemployed teenagers, farmers, and shopwomen, but the busy, narrow streets of Ennis still swarm with people more interested in talking than buying. The streets are still twisting and narrow, full of numerous side alleys and hidden passageways, so that Ennis is one of those rural Irish towns in which you may see familiar faces at every turn and pass the same person three times in the course of a morning. The smell of warm loaves and fresh creamcakes emanates from the bakeries on Parnell and O'Connell streets. Butchers stand at their doors in the early morning as the first cars purr down streets that are no wider than lanes. There's a homely feeling to the place. Among the shops of Ennis are still some of the old general stores, combination hardware-drapery-haberdashery-hosiery-bicycle-seeds-and-everything-else shops. They're "one-stop shopping" from the days before shops became supermarkets and everything came in a plastic bag. Here, behind the counter, a huge roll of brown paper hangs from the wall and twine is pulled seemingly endlessly from some invisible place below.

We were inside the first shop we tried two minutes when a sixty-year-old man in a blue shopcoat walked over to us.

"Lovely day again, thank God," he said, rubbing his hands softly together.

"Yes," I said, smiling and looking down at the rows of shiny children's Wellingtons that had been stacked opposite the door.

"Ah, isn't he a lovely little fellow," he said, holding out a finger for Deirdre to grab onto.

"Do you hear that, Deirdre?"

"Everyone thinks she's a boy," explained Chris pleasantly, hooshing the baby up on her arm.

"It's because she's so strong, God bless her," said the shopman smartly, staying with us as we all moved together toward the back of the store. Above us, the ceiling was hung with a thousand odds and ends, an uncategorizable compendium of things: ten grass clippers tied together, gardening gloves, lengths of chain of different gauges, fishing rods, plastic thimbles set in a piece of bright cardboard, a string bag of footballs, a child's guitar, a series of bicycle wheels and half a dozen pumps rubber-banded in a bunch. The shelves were likewise stocked, and pillows and blankets gave way to cups and saucers, kettles and pots, electric heaters, gas heaters, fan heaters, lengths of fabric, vinyl, small carpets, brush mats, brush heads, and hot water bottles. The eye flickered over everything in amazement, stopping nowhere except perhaps to gaze admiringly at the man in whose head all this was precisely cataloged. He was still playing with Deirdre's finger when we reached the heaters.

"I wonder," I said, almost not wanting to disturb him in his fun, "if you have anything for dampness."

"I have," he said, smiling at Deirdre and not looking up. He went striding off to come back quickly with a small can of something in his hand.

"There you are," he said and resumed his game with the baby.

"What's that?" asked Chris.

"That's for dampness," he said.

I held the tiny plastic bowl of stuff in one hand and asked, "Have you ever heard of something called a dehumidifier?"

There was a long pause in which he looked at me without the slightest expression crossing his face.

"I have," he said almost in reflex, but without the tiniest sign of recognition. It was almost as if while his mouth said the words the poor man was dashing frantically through the amassed stocks in his brain, turning over the myriad dusty boxes of clothes irons, electric knives, weighing scales, and typewriters to try and root out one with the word *dehumidifier* on it. A little time passed, his blank face remained blank, but again he said, "I have."

"It's a machine that dries out dampness," I offered, helpfully.

"Oh yes?" he said. "Yes, well, that's the stuff for dampness there in your hand. That's the best thing for it."

Chris looked at the blue plastic bowl holding white saltlike granules and Deirdre reached out to touch it.

"You see, she knows," chuckled the shopman. "That's the best thing for dampness."

It seemed useless to try and explain that what we had been hoping for was something a little larger to dry out a room. "Well, I suppose we could try it," said Chris.

Taking the package from her hand, the shopkeeper marched up to his counter and, penciling the price into his ledger, pulled off a sheet of brown paper to start wrapping. He didn't use Scotch tape. I watched his practiced hands draw the twine and whirr about the item, little-fingering the knot while he tied up the parcel. When he had done he held it up for Deirdre like a toy.

"I suppose," I ventured, "you've never heard of something called a futon?"

"Ah, yes," he said, making smiling faces at the baby. "I'd say they'd have them at Maguire's."

"Maguire's?" I said, hardly believing our luck. "Which is Maguire's?"

"You know, right next door," he said, "I'd say they have those things there. Sure they have all that class of thing. Fiji and Fuji and that."

I looked at Chris, she looked at me. It was only then we realized: Maguire's was a film and camera shop!

Today we met Paddy Cotter in the village and asked him for his advice on damp-proofing the cottage walls.

"Paddy," I said, "what's the best thing to do about those brown stains that keep coming through the white paint? I got this oil paint stuff in Ennis and it doesn't seem to be making any difference. You can still see the stains."

Paddy said nothing at first. But I could see that a laugh seemed to be traveling around somewhere inside of him looking to get out. "I'll tell you," he said, "but you'll hardly believe me. The only thing to do to put a stop to those stains is to paint the walls . . . with cow-dung!"

I was not tempted to follow this advice.

The garden is in great blossom. The days of August have been warm and dry and have rewarded the two years of Chris's planning and dreaming with an abundance of color splashed right outside the kitchen window. We look out mornings on a tapestry of yellows and purples, greens and blues and reds as the closely intergrown plants of the flower borders paint a path of blossom to the fuchsia hedge. Over breakfasts in August I remembered Chris's spring maps of the garden, what was to be moved, pruned, split, and planted and how little round circles on a white sheet of paper had now become this: the garden in flower. It was deeply satisfying: the print of an imagination upon a small landscape. It was not so much the taming of the wild weedy place that gladdened us, but the released life of the garden, once moribund, now blooming like crazy.

In Manhattan the seasons had swept by us like fast-forward films of racing clouds and falling leaves, glimpsed and gone in moments. Here the tiniest opening of new buds seemed inextricably part of our awareness. To Chris and to me, after two wet summers of muddy soil and rain-pummeled, droopy flowers, the garden in July and August was a triumph. The previous February we had decided that we would try to use only organic fertilizers on the garden, and in the early spring had painstakingly brought barrows of mixed chicken droppings and turf dust from the hen's cabin, liberally dressing the plants with the stuff. It had worked. The lupins and perennial larkspur that grew to six feet did extremely well and suffered no loss of blossom at the expense of growth. We took turns holding Deirdre in our arms in the garden, pointing out the wild yarrow and cornflowers that mingled like clouds in a blue sky. But it was the deep burgundy–colored pompoms of the dahlias that drew her attention. Gardeners everywhere know the joy of this, I thought, of seeing flowers work their magic in a child's eyes.

By mid-August however some of the other costs of organic farming had made themselves known to us. In the vegetable garden there had been an invasion of caterpillars. Not wanting to spray the cabbages with poison, Chris had consulted various organic gardening books for advice. "'Saucers of Guinness left out overnight will attract and drown slugs,'" she read out to me, "but for caterpillars they say to wash each plant with soap, or else just pick them off individually. Yuk!"

So we carried buckets of soapy water from the kitchen to the cabbages the next morning. For a day we had insect-free plants, but a light rain shower that evening undid an hour's work, washing the plants clean and bringing hordes of wriggling green caterpillars back onto the leaves by sunrise. There was nothing for it but to surrender the plants to the insects or pick them off one by one. We had already lost the brussels sprouts to the invasion. Now Chris was determined to save the hundred cabbages that we had carefully set out. In early morning and late evening, Chris went about them, swallowing her utter distaste for the wriggling, crawling creatures, stooping through the cabbage rows and filling old jam jars with a greeny yellowy morass of brassica eaters. Without the heart simply to crush them to a pulp, and uncertain as to how far a caterpillar could travel, she daily carried the jar to a ditch beyond the garden in the hope the insects might not manage to find their way back.

Meanwhile, another of our experiments in the garden seemed to flourish. Chris had read with some excitement a new gardening tip for the growing of potatoes: potatoes laid out on the ground and covered with a sheet of black plastic would grow considerably quicker than those buried underground. Furthermore, with the plastic covering the soil and blocking out the light, no weeds would grow. None whatsoever! All you had to do was snip holes in the covering when the first shoots of the potato tubers started to lift the plastic. What's more, it was an ideal way to make use of a patch of waste or weedy ground that might otherwise stay useless. Much to our neighbors' amazement, in the first week of May, I laid out five rows of Kerr Pink seed potatoes on a small plot of ground infested with the roots of scotch grass and Japanese knotweed. I placed each potato out carefully on the soil, and laid a leftover sheet of black plastic from the previous year's silage cover over them. Within a couple of weeks the first tubers were up, poking through into the light.

"Fine healthy stalks on them, alright," said Joe from

down the road, standing on the path to gaze at them. "You just put them down on the earth, is that it?"

"That's it, Joe. I gave them a little dung, but there's no digging ridges, no earthing them up, no digging them up. When you want a few spuds for the dinner you just pull up a corner of the plastic, reach in, and take out what you want."

"You just take out what you want," he said quietly and looked over at the stalks impassively. "You just reach in and take out what you want," he said again, and walked slowly away.

One evening at the beginning of September I went out before dinner to test the first of the "plastic potatoes," as we called them. They had grown about a month quicker than the main crop of traditionally planted potatoes set in ridges down the eastern side of the garden. Their stalks had been magnificent, they looked like picture-perfect tubers. Bending down to lift a corner of the plastic, I reached my hand under the cover for the first time. Blindly, my fingers felt their way across the cloying moist warm soil until they touched the first potato. I could hardly believe it: the potato was huge! It was as long and as wide as my hand, and for a moment, drawing it out from under the plastic, I felt a thrill of exhilaration. Imagine, we might have grown the first plastic potatoes in all of west Clare, we might have changed forever the way our neighbors would grow their spuds from now on and, with these great enormous balls of potatoes, made some kind of contribution to gardens all around us. All this flashed before me as I drew out the first spud. In the evening light I held it before me, then let out a groan. The whole thing was pocked with holes like a Swiss cheese. Slugs! The second one was the same, and the third. Huge, healthy potatoes, all riddled with holes! Drawing back the whole plastic sheet in one desperate gesture, I saw the entire crop of gorgeous Kerr's Pinks lying there on the soil, not one of them suitable for eating.

Finally, I've started another canvas. Since Deirdre's arrival on June 30 there hasn't been much time for painting. Not that I've minded. She actually takes less time than I expected. It seems like from the moment we got her I've been waiting for the crying, the getting up during the night. But it hasn't happened. Still there is a lot to do with a small baby. And, even on days when there is a snatch of time in which to paint or write, the inspiration isn't there. But today we made time because the day was beautiful and I felt I had to resume, try painting *and* being a mother at the same time.

This new painting is of the flower garden and cottage with two windows. It has taken two full summers to get me out here, but these days are beautiful. I set up my easel on the path beside the lupins and started to paint. I hadn't been at it long when Una, Colette, and Evelyn Downes came through the gate. They come often these days to see Deirdre. Una, especially, is eager to see the baby, being just past the baby age herself. The Downes girls are beautiful. Colette loves to watch me paint and Evelyn is always quizzing me on the names of the flowers, telling me the names of the ones she already knows. Una, with her yellow curls, just watches everything, shyly and sweetly. But the image of the little girls standing around me while I sit on my stool painting the lupins that are taller than all of us nearly brings tears to my eyes. I think of how lucky Deirdre will be to grow up with the outdoors all around her, standing beside the tall, straight spires of the lupins with their starlike leaves. What will she be thinking of, I wonder. What is little Una thinking now when she reaches her hand to stroke the pillars of color that tower above her?

Our parish is full of Michaels. When Chris and I first arrived in Kiltumper, it was something of a joke between us, like one of those awful stage-Irish stories in which Mick says to his brother Pat who says back to Mick, and so on, forever. Michael, Mike, Mick, Mehaul, Mikey, and Mickey: the place is thronged with them, a circumstance easily explained by the fact that our village, Kilmihil, literally means the church of St. Michael, the Archangel. In our first two years here, we have grown quite used to these various derived appellations and try to call no one Mick who is really a Mikey, nor hail a man as Mike who goes by the full name Michael. It's a tricky business, of course, and who knows how often we may have spoken of Mick Considine or Mickey Brew, when we were really referring to their cousins, Mikey Considine and Michael Brew!

Given this superabundance of Michaels, it is easy to imagine the importance of Michaelmas in Kilmihil. This year the feast was celebrated with even greater ceremony, for it marked the fiftieth anniversary of the construction of

St. Michael's Shrine below the graveyard on the road into the village. The shrine, a lovely quiet place with a blessed well, relief statuettes of the stations of the cross built into the wall, and a stone altar, was the scene of an annual outdoor mass and a place where Father Tom, the parish priest, and other parishioners often went to pray in the very early morning or late afternoon. It is an extraordinary place in its own right. It is just off the main road opposite Sean Fitzpatrick's pub, but once you pass through the small gate-turnstile you are in another place altogether. The fifty years of prayers said there seem to have somehow worked themselves into the very stones and air. The well itself is centuries old, and, as I read in the wonderful *Parish of Kilmihil* history book—a book tirelessly put together by some of the ladies in the local Irish Coun-, trywomen's Association, in particular, Annette Collins, Marian Moran, and Maura Cotter—it had curious beginnings. As Annette Collins tells it:

"Reputed to be about the year 1632 AD, a Mrs. Mary MacGorman of Tullycrine dreamt on three successive nights that if she came to Kilmihil Church, she would find a clump of rushes on the southern end of the Church grounds and if these were dug, water would gush forth and on drinking this water, she would be cured. On arrival at the medieval church at Kilmihil (now the ruined church in the cemetery), the colt on which she was riding moved aside into marshy ground nearby, and picked up a mouthful of grass; the whole dripping tuft came away and the colt shook his head—as a horse will to get rid of soil adhered to a tuft—and in doing so sprinkled some drops of water on Mrs. MacGorman, whereupon she was instantly cured of gout and other afflictions from which she had long intensely suffered. Then she, with her son Tom, went to see the then parish priest of Kilmihil, Father Dermot

O'Quealy, who, according to tradition, was also cured of some disease. News of this strange discovery and of its power to effect cures went far and wide and many thousands flocked to the well."

In the *Parish of Kilmihil* I came upon a fading black-and-white photograph of the opening of the shrine fifty years before. There they were, hatted women and bareheaded men, their faces peering out from history at half a century of Irish change in which prayers at the Shrine of St. Michael have remained a constant.

In the last days of September an early winter hush seemed to descend as the village prepared to settle into the long wait for spring. Gone now were the bustling tractor days of mid- and late summer, and the hundred trailer-loads of hay that had come home along west Clare roads with children and women atop them looking down to neighbors and passersby with the satisfaction of seeing the end of another farming year. Traditionally, if there was a goose to be killed it would be killed this week. In old Ireland, Michaelmas was a feast of sharing, of giving to the poor.

This year, for every day of the week leading up to St. Michael's Day, two daily masses were held at the shrine. Seats were brought from the community hall; P. J. Lernihan (over seventy years of age and the man behind concert, ceili, and drama amplification in the village since the days of the first spool tape recorders) wired the loudspeakers. Two short plastic sheets were hung to one side of the altar for protection against the westerly rain. The Legion of Mary organized fresh flowers.

As the day drew nearer, the weather turned wild. Great gusty winds came off the sea and rain clattered on the corrugated roofs of the haybarns where the harvest had been saved. There were heavy showers and rainbows.

Day and night, people came from every hill and townland to sit or stand inside the little gate and hear the
prayers of the mass wavering through the loudspeaker
onto the whistling breeze. On the morning of St. Michael's
Day itself, Chris and I stood there among them. It was a
kind of parish Thanksgiving day. Father Leenane walked
through the crowd, shaking hands and greeting the
schoolchildren. "You're all very welcome here to the
shrine today. I wonder how many of you were here fifty
years ago at the opening ceremony?" he asked. "I wonder,
could we just have a show of hands of anyone who was here
that day? I'm told it was as cold as this one. Does anyone
remember?" Down through the congregation many men
and women raised their hands.

There they were once more, standing in the open
air below the old graveyard, hats and coats bundling
them up as they raised their hands for fifty years in the
village, fifty years of springs and harvests, of births and
deaths, of sick cows, new calves, of good turf, bad turf,
cold winters, wet winters, fifty years of sons and daughters
growing up and moving away, of letters from America, of
seeing the horse and plow become the new tractor become
the old tractor, of living and enduring and prevailing in all
kinds of weather in the same house on the same few fields.
As they raised their hands that morning, I thought: What
stuff these people are made of! When they lowered their
hands a bitter rain slanted in over the graveyard, and
Father Leenane, opening his arms wide, said: "God was
here that day to see the opening of this shrine to St.
Michael. And now, as we finish this week of devotion with
a final mass, God is here with us again today. Let us
pray . . ."

As the rain stung on my face and the murmuring of
prayers was blown back and forth on the wind, the echo of
those words reverberated: God is here with us today.

Deirdre Breen (whom I can no longer simply call Deirdre with wee Deirdre now around) has come for her third visit to Kiltumper. What a trooper. Big Deirdre is so delighted to see Little Deirdre, and she's only here for a week so I hope the weather holds. Deirdre hasn't seen Ireland sunny yet. We have no plans except to enjoy being together. WeeDee, as my sister calls her, is cooing and laughing and talking up a storm lying on her back in the playpen. She's just turned four months and, as they say around here, is a perfect dote! She sleeps through the night, takes two naps during the day, and laughs when she's awake. But she's not one for being on her belly. She starts to cry when I leave her on her belly. In fact, it's practically the only time she cries. I made her a mobile the other day with a blue rubber hanger and pink and green embroidery thread and a champagne cork, a green plastic circle, a blue plastic wing nut for taking studs out of football boots, and a red plastic thing-a-ma-jig. She loves to watch it whirl around and around and around.

We decided to rear turkeys again this autumn and got four of them yesterday. We're going to keep two for ourselves and give one each to Lucy and Tessie for Christmas. Four little white baby turkeys. We threw in some wood shavings and left them alone in the cabin for a day to settle. Now that we're "old hands" at raising poultry, albeit on a very small scale, I no longer feel so attached to them. These are for the table, I say to myself, so don't go making pets out of them. There isn't much to fear on that score as turkeys are not very affectionate anyway! Certainly not like the baby calves in the back meadow. When the first calf was born I used to go out into the big back meadow to where she was lying and sit down beside her. Her mother, Susie, eventually realized that I was only trying to make friends and left us alone. But Niall said that Susie might think I was usurping her position as provider and might reject her calf. So I had to abandon my friendship and watch her sadly from the wall of the back meadow. There'll be nothing like that with the turkeys, I tell myself. I won't feel a thing for them. And yet, going out every morning to let the sunlight pour in over them, I can't resist going gobble-gobble-gobble and watching them swirl up, fluttering their white feathers everywhere in a fever of mad excitement.

There hadn't been a wedding in Kiltumper in ten years and now, finally, there was going to be a grand one. Martin Hehir, our neighbor down the road, and the only young bachelor in the entire townland, was engaged to be married. It was great good news, and greeted with excitement by all our neighbors, for not only was it to be the first Kiltumper wedding for quite some time, it also meant new life in the townland. In these days, when our parish loses great numbers of its young people to emigration every year, and all over the West we see the ruins and shells of abandoned cottages, the prospect of a young man marrying and making a go of living in west Clare is cause enough for gladness.

From the first, after the news of the wedding was announced, as plans were made to hire a minibus to take all our neighbors to the reception in Ennis, there was talk of a *Bacachs*.

Bacachs (pronounced baa-hox) was a word I had never heard until I came to Clare, and it was only gradually that I came to understand the ancient festive ritual that was bound up in it. I said it but couldn't spell it, and for a couple of days found no one who could explain it to me. "It's an old tradition around here, Niall," explained Mary one day. "*Bacachs* is like strawboys," she said.

"Strawboys?" I said, no wiser than before.

"You'll see," she said with a sudden smile coming over her. "At Martin's we'll have a *Bacachs,* please God. You might even see some eye-fiddles!"

"Eye-fiddles, Mary?"

"You know, things over your face so as they wouldn't know you, masks-like. We call them eye-fiddles," she said and laughed at the incredulous look on my face.

I thought to myself of the marvelous aptness of the name eye-fiddles, literally things which fiddled the eye. It was another little while before I found out more. At country weddings in west Clare, on the night of the wedding feast itself, or on the night on which the bride and bridegroom returned to their house after a honeymoon, a number of their neighbors would disguise themselves using straw, costumes and eye-fiddles. The men would dress as women and vice versa, and together in disguise they would arrive at the newly married couple' house after dark. One of them would carry a stick and would sweep into the room before the others, quietening the visitors who were there and settling the room for the beginning of the *Bacachs.* Then, with the starting up of some ceili music, the Straw-boys would suddenly enter the room and start to dance a Clare set, a traditional dance consisting of two jigs, two reels, and a hornpipe. Then, while all who were seated tried to puzzle out the true identities of the dancers in disguise, the bride would be drawn up into the dance and whisked around the room in the company of these characters in their eye-fiddles. It was a thing of great merriment and fun and supposed to bring luck to the newlyweds. When the set was over the little group of the *Bacachs* would depart at once, quite often to return to the feast shortly thereafter in their ordinary clothes and dance the rest of the feast away.

What we knew of the *Bacachs* up until Martin's wedding had been gathered from tales told by our neighbors and a few scholarly articles in books in the library. It was at first hard to believe that the tradition still existed. But when the day finally came for Martin and Pauline to be married, and we sat in Ennis at a long, fabulously spread table with all our neighbors, the word was in the air. James, Martin's brother from Dublin, had whispered it to Mary: "Is there going to be a *Bacachs* in Kiltumper?" "There is," she said. Plans quickly got under way. The newlyweds would be returning from their honeymoon in a fortnight. James would send word to Mary when they were on their way and Mary would alert the others. From Ballynacally, Mrs. Hehir would arrive and from Ennis Pauline's family would come with the makings of the feast between them.

For two weeks while Martin and Pauline honeymooned in the sun of Europe, the *Bacachs* kept cropping up in conversation around the fires of Kiltumper. Previous episodes of strawboys were remembered gleefully. "Well Michael Dooley is a pure circus at it," said Mary, giggling to herself as she told us. "He'd put on some old skirt on him. Well, he'd make you laugh so he would." And laugh we did, just sitting there imagining the whole thing taking shape.

We could hardly wait. True to his word, on the day the newlyweds arrived back in Dublin and set off on the road down to Clare, James Hehir called Mary. The plan was simple: Martin and Pauline would arrive in Kiltumper in the early evening. They'd come into their house and find all quiet. Then, little by little, visitors would arrive. Meanwhile, gathering at Mary's house down the road, Michael and Breda Dooley, Michael and Pauline Downes, Paul and Kathleen O'Shea, and Joeso Breen and Josie would put on their disguises, wait until the evening was well along, then set forth to Hehirs' *Bacachs*.

The night was cloudy and moonless. Down in Mary's big kitchen old pants and skirts and pajamas were taken from the cupboards. In a giddy mood of excitement, chuckling to himself, Michael Dooley rolled up his trouser legs and pulled on an old pair of tights. "Look at the grand legs on him," said Josie, Mary's aunt and a marvelous, lively woman of over seventy who was staying with Mary. "Give me a look at that one," said Michael Downes, taking a gaudy purple dress from Paul and holding it up to him. "I think this is my style alright," he said, grinning. Mary burst out laughing as she stepped into a second pair of striped men's pajamas. "Well, I look like a right ol' elephant," she said, laughing out loud. "You do, faith," said Josie, "and two of 'em!"

There were green hats, red shirts, blue housecoats, orange blouses, mismatched old clothes all over the place as everyone entered into the spirit of the thing. There were nylons and tights for covering faces, and veils and scarves, too. "Mind that now," said Michael Downes as Paul stuffed an ever more enormous bosom inside the top of a black-and-white dress embroidered with hearts. "You want to be careful of that," he joked, "you could get mastitis!"

When they were finally ready it was near midnight, and as they hurried down the road to Hehirs' there was rain on the night wind. Outside the door the weird-looking little group of the *Bacachs* gathered themselves in whispers for their entrance. Bernadette Dooley, drawing her scarf up over her face, burst into the kitchen and set the music. Then, to the lively playing of a spirited jig, the Kiltumper *Bacachs* came in dancing. There were whoops and giggles, applause, and shouted guesses as they twirled and whirled, drawing Pauline, the bride, up into the dance and whisking her round her own kitchen to the jigging of Irish music. The house was alive with it. It was past midnight and just getting into full swing. Michael Garvey had his flute, a goat-skin *bodhran* drum was brought out, and John Joe Russell played his tin whistle. The music was magical. The *Bacachs* were supposed to finish the set and go out into the dark to change into their own clothes. But before they had time, another crowd of callers arrived and asked them to come in again and perform again. And so they did. There was more dancing and more laughing. Another group of *Bacachs* from Ennis arrived and took over the kitchen with another Clare set. A great table of food was discovered laid out in the parlor, with two roasted turkeys, hills of sandwiches, hot tarts, scones and cakes of all kinds. The whole house filled up with well-wishers. The lights burned on, the jigs and reels carried into the wind, and to the sounds of neighbors laughing and applauding, as dance after dance ended, a newly married couple's life in Kiltumper began.

CHAPTER SIX _____

How was it all going, then?

It was going just fine. The cows and calves were thriving on the hill fields, Upper and Lower Tumper, at the back of the house, the turkeys were gathering weight by the day, and the new hens were laying. Deirdre was still sleeping through the night and filling the cottage with the soft gurgling sounds of first baby talk by day. Chris had again found the time to paint and a bright canvas of flowers and light hung in the parlor. We had both found time to write. And in two weeks we were going to return to New York for the publication of our first book.

It was for all of this that we came here, I thought to myself as I went up to check on the animals in the stilly greeny light of a late September evening. I loved to stand there looking west to the sliver of ocean and down to the plume of turf smoke rising from the cottage into the night sky. Our life had changed almost beyond recognition, I thought. And suddenly the prospect of my first trip back to Manhattan since leaving for Kiltumper was tinged with anxiety. Chris had been back once already and looked forward to another trip "home" with the excitement of a child about to embark on a shopping spree in F.A.O. Schwarz's. But I wondered how fragile and unreal a thing was our life here. Had we really built ourselves a pastoral idyll, albeit a rainy one? In the hot white light of New York would it measure up? There was another reason for anxiety, too; we would be leaving Deirdre behind. As she was not yet legally adopted, we couldn't take her out of the country and, although we knew there was no better place for her than with Lucy, Larry, and their children down in the village, we worried about her reaction. Would we be risking the new bond that had grown so steadily among all three of us? We felt simple guilt at leaving her, as well. We thought of it, felt it, and worried. Then for a few days we were caught up in the quickening pace of activities around the farm. But late at night with Deirdre sleeping soundly in the back room, we stood at the door and looked in on her and worried some more.

With the last days of summer came a slightly different, autumnal feeling to life in Kiltumper. There was an end-of-summer rhythm now that seemed to hasten everything to conclusion before the rains of winter. This was part of the rhythm of our lives now, this hasty, last-minute getting ready for winter. It was so tangled up with every day's slightly cooler breeze and earlier sunset that it seemed to me there was a full and natural connection now between ourselves and the life of the farm. It was *not* only part of our life, we were part of *it*, too. A brisk wind tossed the sycamore leaves into a scratchy dance at the back door and

I thought *that* wind is one of the last dry winds of summer, we must bring home our turf before the rain.

At the end of September, we carried Deirdre up the hill fields of Tumper and across the Bog Meadow to inspect our turf. As always, we were a little behind our neighbors. Great reeks, or stacks, of turf could already be seen in cabins and haybarns around the townland, and in the shops in the village people had stopped asking: "Have you the turf home?" Instead, the talk was: "Wasn't it a great summer for the hay and the turf?" I said it was, and made no mention of the fact that our winter's fuel was still on the bog. It had been footed and refooted, and so on the day after we showed Deirdre her first sod of dry black turf, I began the business of bagging it. Each of over a thousand pieces, which had already been handled and rehandled six or seven times, was now put into a plastic fertilizer bag and the bags carried across the spongy bogland to a place where they could be loaded into a tractor. In order to bring it home from the bog we were counting on our neighbors' help. But first I had to fill the bags, working to the pulse of the autumn rhythm in the air, sensing the stiffening breeze, the less-blue sky, and the vivid trembling of the last leaves on the trees. It was two windy days' work, trudging back and forth among the purple spires of the heather and the weathered bracken, watching the little heap of bagged turf rise into something of a mound. There was not a soul nor the sound of a soul anywhere. I sang snippets of songs out loud to myself and said half-remembered lines of Irish poems. A white-tailed hare, traveling between the top meadow and the forestry, froze at a spot thirty yards from me. He lifted his head and seemed to eye me, then was gone, tearing across a horizon that had darkened with storm. The top surface of the bog had already begun to soften and puddle from the first few rains of September. My Wellingtons sank deep and marked a trail across the face of the brown bog. We had cut plenty of turf this year, and it was all dry, and in every bag filled I felt the warmth of the wintering cottage and saw the image of Deirdre in her bath before the fire. Still, if rain came, the bags of turf would be marooned there on the bog. That night the air drizzled but didn't rain. And by six on the following evening, dragging the final bags from the far corner of the turf bank, I heard the sputtering of Michael's tractor with a trailer coming up the fields. Neither Chris nor I had asked him. But as he saluted and his son, Francie, waved, I realized there had been no need to.

Summer is gone.

It has been a good year in the garden. As the autumn perennials come into bloom and the last of the annuals lingers on I am able to measure the success of my third summer garden. After all, there is much to admire since that first summer when the nasturtiums and montbretia, too bountiful, emblazoned the garden path like an orange sun ray and the towering, threatening nettles stood like enemy guards holding everything captive. Now the path, a carousel of color, is bordered with oriental poppies, dahlias, delphiniums, even goldenrod, which they sell here as a perennial. The front garden border just in front of the house has expanded to both sides of the center path. Bit by bit, we are reclaiming the soil and wresting it from the weeds. In the vegetable plots, the sugar snap peas—this time Deirdre Breen had sent the dwarf variety, whose tiny tenacious tendrils secured themselves easily to the pea fence—have been abundant. The weather was warm enough for French beans and they thrived in their bed of turf dust. And for the first time, the carrots grew! Carrots have never grown well in this soil, Mary has told me time and again. But this year, I concentrated much effort on sifting the soil and added enough sand and turf dust so they could thrive. The soil here in west Clare is called gleys. It's nearly impenetrable because of the thick, stodgy clay particles that hang together so tightly even water cannot drain. It's ideal for growing rushes, a characteristic vegetation in west Clare that renders the land 'severely disadvantaged' under the E.E.C. Agricultural Policy. I often find rushes growing in the garden in soil which is wet and solid and needs total reconstitution. But, still, inch by inch, we are making Kiltumper's garden into a "cottage garden" and the rewards this fine summer have been worth all the effort.

Today Deirdre had her developmental test down at the Kilmihil Clinic. The Mid-Western Health Board sends around a doctor every couple of months to the individual clinics to examine babies around the age of six months. Deirdre is five and a half months and was called for an appointment. The service is free and offered only once, so we decided to go and see what it was all about. The lady doctor and Mrs. Carey, our local nurse, together checked Deirdre for hip displacement, they weighed her and asked about her food intake. They checked her reflexes and measured her head. They put her on the floor to see if she could crawl and we watched her move her right arm out and pivot on her belly in the beginnings of a circle. The doctor said that is how most babies begin to crawl—by moving in a circle. Then they checked her hearing. Deirdre was sitting squarely on my lap facing the nurse, a large and jovial woman and mother of five, who was holding a tiny, naked rubber doll out to Deirdre trying to distract her and keep her looking straight ahead. Meanwhile, the doctor held a small rattle to one side of Deirdre's head and shook it. The sound was tiny but audible and I saw it register with Deirdre but she made no effort to turn around to look at it. No, she was too busy watching the big nurse with the tiny doll. The doctor shook it again and again and when Deirdre finally turned to it, she had this look on her face that seemed to say, "All right, already, I hear you." I laughed at her. She is so funny and so very alert. The doctor said she was perfect and very observant. Sure, I knew that, I said to myself and went home to Niall with my little perfect princess pie.

Notes from America, *Friday, October 16.*

The incredible speed of it all. Six hours and suddenly all the green fields on the almost limitless horizon of Kiltumper are replaced by a long white corridor in the Arrivals building of Kennedy Airport. "Americans, this way," a black woman in a blue uniform chants cheerlessly over the heads of three planeloads of passengers, and suddenly Chris has left me. Clutching my Irish passport, I stand in line for immigration control and feel a tightening dread sweep over me. Here and there among a long line of Algerian and German passengers, I can spot my countrymen and women easily. So many of them, with faces freckled by the Irish summer, standing there in their Sunday best, hoping a tourist visa will slip them past the guards into America. In that fluorescent-lit and air-conditioned place you wait in a no-man's land somewhere between the dole queues of rural Ireland and the rich promise of New York. Behind the control cubicles an immigration guard stands watching; upon his hip he wears a gun and a truncheon. For all the talk of Ulster and the Troubles I have never seen a handgun in Ireland. Inching ahead in the queue I look down and see the green cover of my passport is printed with the sweat of my fingers.

When my turn eventually comes, I'm nervous for no reason at all. I have a Resident Alien green card (actually mine is blue) inside the cover of my passport, but the inscrutable lady inside the glass cubicle still chills me. I try to look at ease as I hand over my papers. She flicks the pages of my passport; my blue card falls out.

"This you?" she says, with a glance at the photograph.

"Yes,"I say, taking off my glasses.

"Doesn't look like you," she says, staring at me steadily.

"It was taken a few years ago. I didn't have a beard then," I tell her nicely, and feel her eyes move to my chin. When she says nothing I'm even further unnerved and stupidly add, "I live in Ireland now, in the countryside, so I don't shave . . ."

"That so," she says, looking into my passport again. "If you live in Ireland how come you got a U.S. Resident Alien card? How long you been outta this country?"

"Just two years."

"Two years?"

"Yes."

"Jesus," she says, and shakes her head angrily at me. Her voice is suddenly louder. I glance at the guard at the back of the cubicle and feel like shrinking into the floor. "This card is invalid. You can't be outta this country two years and keep a blue card. A blue card is for residents!"

"I was a resi . . ."

"Listen," she says, taking my passport and getting up out of her seat, "don't you move from that spot, you hear me?"

I try not to move from that spot. I try not to look back at

the people in the line behind me as the angry lady with my passport leaves her post and disappears into the nexus of immigration offices. It's a few moments before she returns. She hasn't got my passport.

"You see that place over there?" she says to me. She's pointing to a zone painted and outlined in red. "You go over there, there's a lady there wants to talk to you."

"Can I have my passport?"

"That lady has your passport," she says without looking at me.

I take one glance at the guard, another at the long line of people waiting behind the white line with their passports, and walk over to the red zone. "Wait there," a man in a blue uniform says, and points to a red plastic bench. I sit down beside a very beautiful woman wrapped from head to toe in assorted white cloths and jabbering to herself in what I take to be a kind of aristocratic Arabic. Apparently she has mistakenly brought her sister's passport all the way from somewhere amidst the sands of Arabia. She doesn't look like the faded bluish photograph and speaks very broken English. I try to shrug my shoulders and nod my head helpfully to her, but this only serves to antagonize her further. When she's brought up to the counter a long discourse in sign language ensues. It's five or ten minutes before the lady behind the counter loses patience and looks straight into the face of the Arab to say, "Honey, you and me need an interpreter here." As the lady in white is escorted somewhere else and a European man in a green leather jacket walks sheepishly into the red zone, I'm called forward.

There's a black woman in another blue uniform behind the counter. She's slowly turning the pages of my passport. "What's your story?" she asks impassively.

"I'm sorry, I didn't know my blue card wasn't valid for life. I thought—"

"You was ignorant of the law," she says. She says it in a way that will brook no disagreement.

"I was," I say.

"You was ignorant of the facts," she says, still not looking up at me.

"I was."

Then, suddenly, she raises her head and stares at me. "That's about the only thing you got going for you. I can send you off to the immigration judge right now and he can send you back wherever you come from, right now, you understand? Right now, he can do that." I nod my head, I understand. *Right back where I come from,* runs through my head; was it only this morning I was out in the cabins feeding the hens and turkeys? Was it only hours ago I took a check around the farm, walking out into the fields and feeling lord of everything?

"I can do that," she says, "I'm entitled to do that. But I'm not going to do that."

"Thank you."

"Because you was ignorant this time, this time I'm going to slap a fifteen-dollar fine on you and grant you a waiver to let you into this country, you understand?"

I say "yes" and "thank you." Standing there before her I feel cold sweat break all over me. I need air, I need to get outside. Just then, reaching for my wallet, I turn and see Chris with the suitcases already loaded onto the trolley, making her way back against the traffic of non-Americans with a worried look on her face. She spots me in the Red Zone and hurries over.

"What's the matter?" she asks me, as she comes up to the counter.

"Nothing. Everything's all right now. I have to pay a fifteen-dollar fine, that's all."

"Why?"

Now isn't the time to get into it, I'm thinking, as the lady behind the counter puts her hands on her hips and looks at us, the hopelessly flustered international travelers in the Red Zone.

From my wallet I draw out a twenty-dollar bill. It is the only American money I have on me, as we haven't had a chance to get to a bank yet.

Seeing it, the lady scowls.

"Haven't you got fifteen? Otherwise I gotta go all the way down the cashier."

"No, I'm sorry," I say, holding my wallet tightly shut and knowing that there's nothing inside it.

"You sure?" says the lady.

"Yes, we have it," Chris suddenly cuts in. "Niall, I saw three fives in the wallet this morning before we left—here, let me see."

In a moment the wallet is on the counter, and I'm trying to stand back a little and look away as the immigration lady is bending over it and seeing that we don't have another dollar in it.

"This *all* the money you got?" she says to me, holding up the twenty before me.

"Yes . . . well no, we have money in—"

"Haven't *you* got any money, honey?" she says to Chris, almost in disbelief.

There is a slight pause. Then:

"No," says Chris, "he's got all of our money."

A few moments later we are walking out of the Red Zone, five dollars in our pocket, and a lady from immigration control shaking her head in amazement at us as we head into the New World. Within minutes we push out into the crowded main concourse. There among the panoramic gallery of faces—more faces than I think I've seen in two years—Chris's cousin Vincent and her brother Sean are watching for us. As we rush outside the building a warm wave of dead air rises over us. It is hotter than summertime in Ireland and as we hurry over to where the car has been been left running, a policeman approaches us, shouting: "That your car? Get that car outta here. You can't leave that car here, get it outta here!"

Vincent holds out his hand to me with a wide grin: "Welcome to America" is what he says.

Saturday, October 17.

An early morning wake-up to doughnuts and coffee in Deirdre and Larry's apartment in New Rochelle. Then, after the glory of an American shower, we are driven to the train station. The very smells and sounds of the train speeding to the platform, and the hiss as the doors open to take us, are the stuff of memory. Here we were, two years previously, going to work with the *New York Times* and a plastic container of coffee with its lid broken off at the mouth. But this is a Saturday morning, the train is half empty. As we sit there rattling into Manhattan for an interview on National Public Radio, I can think of no place farther from the open spaces of Kiltumper. How is Baby Deirdre at Lucy's this morning? I'm wondering, and wish we had been able to bring her with us. How are the hens and the turkeys? How are Susie, Gerty, and Phoebe and their calves on the slopes of Upper Tumper? Dreaming such things, I look out and see the familiar dark tunnel approach of Grand Central Station. We are under the city now and slowing down. A moment later, the carriage lights go out, then flicker back on as the train grinds to a stop in the tunnel, about one underground mile from the platform. A man groans and his friend makes a joke and we all sit there for a while going nowhere. Ten minutes pass. Chris turns to me with a face that remembers so many scenes like this. "Isn't this terrible," she says, "and there's absolutely nothing we can do. We're going to be late now."

Another ten minutes pass in the cavernous dark, and we begin to feel trapped there, sitting anxiously in our seats. A voice from the speaker on the wall tells us the computer signal system is out of order. We can't move forward to the platform until we get the word. The man who groaned earlier now yells an obscenity. "I can't believe this," says Chris, caught between laughing and crying. After another few minutes the train jolts into motion *and backs away from the station out of the tunnel!* The whole carriage is full of a simmering anger now, and on this, our first trip back into the Big Apple, it begins to seem like we'll never get there. I close my eyes, breathe deeply, and think only of the salt sea crashing on the west coast of Clare.

An hour later we are sitting in a National Public Radio sound studio on East 34th Street. From Washington, Lynn Neary is asking us why we decided to leave Manhattan and move to Ireland. We are both still thinking of that morning's train ride, but as we talk of Kiltumper, the very saying of the words, the telling about the green fields in summer light, and the conjuring of all the country images of our life there in the wind and rain, bring sweeping over us that "Irish feeling." And as we are drawing ourselves back into it, there is a sudden interruption. On the line from Moscow is a front-page news story, someone else who left America for another life in another country—the first-ever U.S. serviceman to defect to Russia! On a crackling staticky line he tells of his hardships in penetrating another culture, of the very different life of rural Russia, where he and his girl friend are living. (Having asked his new compatriots for a job working with exotic animals, he has been given a position handling snakes in the wastes of Georgia!) His story is long and confusing, but in the end we understand that he cannot return to America and isn't happy in Russia and is currently awaiting permission to move to East Germany! A man without a country or a home. Listening to him makes us grateful for our own good fortune, for in many ways, we have two countries to call home. I know New York will always be the place Chris first thinks of as home, and as for me, Ireland is mine. It adds an edge of adventure to our life together, in many ways endowing us with a sense of freedom to live almost anywhere. It is not, however, without its snags, and as Lynn Neary ends the interview her last question is answered by both of us at the same time. "So, tell me," she asks, "will you be staying in Ireland forever?" My "yes" and Chris's "no" are simultaneous, and turning to one another we break into laughter.

Sunday, October 18.

We both wake early in the welcome comfort of Chris's mother's condominium in northern Westchester. It's a dazzling blue autumn day, and already, after only two days here, we are both eager to walk in open spaces. We slip out across the patio to the manicured rolling grass of the golf course and set off, walking silently beneath the red and gold of oak leaves. The light is fantastic and the air clear and honeycombed with leaves; only the slight purr of distant cars makes the sleeping day wake. When we come back Chris's mother and her grandfather, Phil O' Connell, have the coffee ready. More important, there on the kitchen table in all its splendor is something we have both continued to miss in Kiltumper: the Sunday *New York Times*.

"Which section would you like to start with, Niall?" asks Chris's mother, sliding the great folded feast of words over to me. She knows I miss this Sunday ritual, and although we have a subscription to the Book Review, courtesy of herself, it's welcome arrival two months late is no substitute for the pleasure of the complete newspaper. This morning I sit and marvel at the monstrous size of the whole paper and wonder at all the news of the world that we haven't been reading in Kiltumper.

Monday, October 19.

Our first full day in Manhattan. This time we commute in on the early train with all the businesspeople, the morning-coffee drinkers, pen-and-calculator men, dictaphone speakers, sports-page readers, sleepers, smokers, and bridge players. The air is sweet with aftershave and perfume. The whole train strikes me as a kind of exclusive club, and sitting with Chris I feel a little giddy at the thought that we have relinquished our membership forever. An hour and a half later, we call at our good friend Charlie's office on East 44th Street. Charlie enjoys talk of distant places and conjuring up the image of himself giving everything up for a life of travel. For a moment I leave Chris telling him of the exotic rains of Kiltumper and step out of his office to find a washroom. Walking down the luxurious carpeted corridor, a man in an elegant white shirt and silk tie looks at me and says hello.

"I don't think I've seen you here before," he says. "You must be the new receptionist on the tenth floor. Welcome."

"Thank you," I say.

"It's a great company, you'll enjoy it here," he says warmly and walks away.

Outside on the streets again, we are like leaves in the wind. We've both lost the New York attitude, and betray ourselves terribly by *looking at things*. New Yorkers don't look, but seem to stride, gliding fast-forward between offices and apartments with the certain knowledge that all around and over them is a city so extraordinarily various that nothing it throws up in front of you is surprising anymore. You simply don't look at the man in the loincloth singing a loud aria as he steps into the chill waters of a Fifth Avenue fountain. You push on to your appointment, moving through streets aromatic with everything from the world's most expensive perfumes to roasted chestnuts, hot dogs and bagels. Windows of dazzling jewels and expensive clothes don't necessarily stun you, for why should they, New Yorkers seem to say, dancing onward between the reflections of light on glass and steel, tenaciously holding to a belief in the possibility of all things. This, more than anything, marks the foreignness of the city for both of us now. It is the thing we are most unused to, this attitude of confidence in the future, of certainty in attaining a goal.

As we walk down Lexington Avenue people keep bumping into us and walking on. We try walking nearer to the shop windows but it's no different. At a stop sign on 34th Street we wait, watching wide cars bellying down the avenue and seeing steam rising out of the street as if from nowhere. Suddenly behind us we see a man in rags with a huge plastic bag of cans on his shoulder. I make the mistake of looking back at him, and, swaying and glaring, he roars out curses at me. The stop light takes a long time to change. A little crowd gathers at the curb and he curses everyone in a stream of foul language. Chris steps down into the street, and even as the light flashes DON'T WALK we hurry across. "I feel as if I have to protect my back all the time," she says.

We are due to meet for lunch with Juris, Laura, Susan, and Alan, the little band of our publishers, but now we decide against walking all the way there. Instead we go down into the subway. Even now, before midday, there seem to be hundreds of people down there, and from the far end of the platform the staccato beat of funk music pumps through the heavy air. We want to go to Wall Street Chris confidently decides, looking at the subway map. When the downtown train pulls in we step onto it feeling as conspicuous as west Clare farmers. Losing my balance slightly, I tip gently against a woman next to me. She looks around without a smile. After a few moments we see that the train is pulling into a station called Brooklyn Bridge. The thought hits both of us at the same time: My God, Brooklyn Bridge, we've gone way too far, we're in Brooklyn! And just as the doors prepare to close, we leap out onto the platform.

It's a few minutes before we ask a man in a three-piece suit which way is Wall Street. "Wall Street?" he says. "That was the next stop on the train you just got off."

Half an hour later we are sitting in a spacious dining room, upstairs at the Downtown Association. Never having heard of it, it strikes me as one of those very civilized places you don't find very often in New York because they are like hidden treasures, and as we sit poised delicately over Nova Scotia salmon, tilefish, and pumpkin pie I am remembering that Jan Morris, the travel writer, has described Manhattan as one of the most civilized places on earth. Coming up from the dark labyrinth of the New York City subway system, with litter and unfortunate sleeping bodies strewn side by side, it seems an extraordinary description. In the evening, sitting with Chris's mother to watch the evening news we learned that that afternoon the New York Stock Exchange suffered the biggest crash in its history. So then, the thought comes to me, a kind of wild and crazy measurement of the city's civilization: among the stockbrokers, businessmen, and lawyers who were sitting quietly at their tables in the dining room of the Downtown Association this afternoon, several million dollars will have been lost between dinner and dessert.

Thursday, October 22.

How is Deirdre? Chris wakes full of restlessness to see her, and before breakfast we call Lucy and Larry, her Irish godparents, in Kilmihil. She is well, we hear, but teething. Does she miss us? We are all too aware of the yet fragile early state of the bonding between the three of us and worry that in some way the baby will feel a resentment towards us. I wish she was with us, or rather, I wish for a moment with her in my arms, the smell and warmth of her, the clasp of her finger around mine, the gurgle of her talk as she points to the dazzling color of a late rose blooming along the garden path. This evening as we fly another six and a half hours farther from her to San Francisco, I am beginning to think it is here and not Kiltumper that is the unreal place.

At eleven o'clock at night we arrive at San Francisco International Airport. Chris's brother Stephen and his wife Danna are waiting for us, and as we move from the terminal to the parking garage, the night air is mild and windless. I have no real idea of where exactly I am; I am following tunnels and yellow lights, and catching for the first of many times in San Francisco the sensation of being somewhere within a carnival. From the trunk of the car, magicianlike at midnight, Stephen takes out a pepperoni pizza. "We thought you might be hungry," he says with a grin.

We are staying tonight in what I am told is the "pool house" at Danna's parents' home in Portola Valley. "Pool house." The words stick in my head, conjuring richly comical images of their like in west Clare. The contrasts are staggering. Pool house, puddle house? Coming down the cobbled steps in the pitch darkness, I can sense the slow lapping of the pool water and suddenly feel a little giddy. If only our neighbors in Kilmihil could see us now.

For her part, Chris feels at home, and for a moment in the starlit darkness I wish for her sake that we could stay for a month. The whole thing is like a dream to me. The lights across San Francisco Bay sit like nests of fallen stars, and as we carry our bags in through the sliding doors my sense of fantasy is doubled when Danna tells me: "You can sleep with the windows open if you like. We haven't had rain here for eight weeks."

Friday, October 23.

Five o'clock in the morning and we startle, awake. Lights are coming on up in the main house. In each room, one after the other, the lights are being switched on. There's a kind of hissing noise in the air, and sitting up in bed I think I can make out the shadow of a woman moving in a dance outside on the lawn past the windowed lights. It goes on for some minutes, the soft noise, the soft lights, and the shadowy dancing. I think I am dreaming and go back to sleep.

It is only later over breakfast that I hear a radio DJ announce that at five o'clock in the morning the Bay area had its first rain in months. It wasn't a dream. It was Ruth Ann—Danna's mother—in celebration, stepping in rhythm to the falling rain in her garden. I can think of no greater measure of the difference between where Chris and I have come from and where we are. Imagine all the rain dances there would have to be in Kiltumper.

Saturday, October 24.

In the Carnival City. Perhaps it is the hills, the roller-coaster cable cars with their vague brush of danger in squealing brakes, racing descents, and the brazen bell rung at the crossroads; perhaps it is the spell of the Pacific Ocean itself, the *westerliness* of the place, the earthquake edge of it, the nowhere-further-to-go quality that seems to invest the streets with an air of care-freedomness and dance; perhaps it's Chinatown and moonlight on the Bay, Italian restaurants, the easy sunlight and swooping fogs. Whatever it is I cannot escape the feeling of carnival here. San Francisco seems to revel in itself, in the blue and flower-scented air; and in the colorful, festive texture of its neighborhoods there seems to be room for everyone. During our five days we gaily partake of the merriment and whirl around the white city without a care in the world.

In the morning sunshine, I bare my pale legs in a pair of shorts for the first time in ages and make jokes for Stephen and Danna's little boys, Ryan and Kellen, about how they'll love the wet sun of Ireland. Danna takes Chris to an exercise class and Stephen throws me a tennis racket.

Only hours later, at the Fog City Diner in San Francisco we are treated to fried oyster sandwiches and quesadillas. I keep trying to pinch myself. In the Compass Rose room of the Saint Francis Hotel, we sip English tea and eat pâté while an unobtrusive string trio plays eighteenth-century music. Ten minutes later, we zoom thirty-two floors in the same building and walk inside an exotic nightclub called Oz. We are at the top of the city. By moonlight we hang from a cable car that grinds up the last hills of night and rushes seaward in the cooling air to the Hyde Street pier. There timber boats rock softly by the South End Rowing Club and the dark-shadowed heads of late-night swimmers bob on the water like seals. Old walrus-men rise up out of the water and walk gracefully to shore. Behind them the hump of Alcatraz, before them the strung lights of the pier at the water's edge, and the rising, glittering hills of the Carnival City.

Monday, October 26.

Kiltumper is drawing near again. Yesterday, Ryan and Kellen let off green helium balloons into the blue sky of

California, and watching them go, floating, to become green dots in space, I was dreaming of the bumpy road west of the cottage where the gorse blossoms yellow in springtime. I am dizzy with America, giddy with lights and scents and sights; tonight I tell my journal that I need to walk our fields in the clean rain and feel grass and rocks and dirt.

Wednesday, October 28.

We are back in autumnal Westchester, driving for the last time the rich yet rural roads behind Katonah, Bedford, and Mount Kisco. These were our first places in married life, they are among Chris's favorite memories, and so today we travel them with the keen nostalgia of people moving through the scenes of childhood. We visit Grenville T. Emmett, the great-grandnephew of the Irish patriot Robert Emmett and a long-standing friend of Chris's family. Chris shows me the fading mural on the wall above his garage on Pea Pond Road where as a child she had first been struck by the magic of art. Walking with a cane, Grenny brings us in for Irish tea and cinnamon toast and, as I realize how closely he resembles the statue of Robert Emmett that stands on St. Stephens Green, I am struck quite forcibly by another image of emigration, and the real and living links between American and Irish history. Upon the wall is a nineteenth century painting of Thomas Addison Emmett and his mother, and just across from it, tightly packed shelves of books on Irish biography and history. "Tell me, Crissie," asks Grenny, with a gleam in his eye, "are there still all those marvelous little old hotels I used to know in Dublin?"

Later, as we drive away through the last light of afternoon, leaves are everywhere, and the mellowness of mood and season fills the fall air with a sense of endings. Dry leaves fly up from beneath cars in great red and golden gusts as rays of sunlight are briefly spangled with color. There is a rare beauty to the afternoon, an incomparable sense of the softly fading light of late autumn. It is as lovely in these moments here as anywhere else on earth, and yet the landscape seems to me to be all outside, untouchable and impenetrable. Fenced, owned, and arranged like a picture. What can I say? Has it been the measure of the effect of Kiltumper upon my spirit that now nothing will do for me but to be inside, part of the landscape itself, moving and breathing within it? We speed on in a hush and I think: tomorrow we'll see morning again over the silvery light of the Shannon and walk up the garden path to resume a quiet life in the hills of Clare.

CHAPTER SEVEN

We landed at Shannon Airport in a gray November dawn and in a single moment seemed to have entered the province of winter. We were back. The bright, warm light and tennis courts of California belonged to a rapidly fading past and as we left the terminal the familiar cool moist air of the West swept over us. I cannot deny that my heart quickened, even as I sensed Chris's stiffening into the breeze. Would it always be so, I wondered. Would I ever step from a plane at Shannon and not feel a little giddy with delight, a little quickstep in my stride? And would Chris always don a brave smile against the rain-thick air?

Our good friend Larry had come to meet us. We were glad to see him. He had risen early in order to greet our six a.m. arrival, and for that we were most grateful. Larry could see by our faces that we were tired and he guessed our emotions were high.

"How'ya, Chris? How'ya, Niall? Welcome back, lads."

There followed a short moment in which we gave each other quick Irish kisses. Emblems of fondness in a shy society. We inquired after all the Blakes and upon hearing that they were all well we asked about Deirdre.

"Deirdre's fine. She had a bit of a cold there last week but she's over it now."

"Did she miss us, Larry?" asked Chris.

There was a moment's pause.

"She did, I'd say."

She did, I'd say. The words echoed in both our minds. We kept quiet and got into the car and were shortly speeding westwards into Clare. Did she really? Did she whimper or roar for us? Or did she not even realize we were gone? Either way we began to feel dread gather within us. Naturally, we wanted her to have missed us a *little* bit. It would undermine our already fragile confidence as new parents if we walked into Lucy and Larry's kitchen and Deirdre simply ignored us. Our minds were preoccupied with misgivings as Larry cheerily asked us about America. We answered vaguely as the car flew and bumped along the winding roads of the west. Fine ribbons of silver mist lay in the valleys. Cows, like sentries to the dawn, stood where they were and watched birds scatter into the gray sky. What an extraordinary peace was here, I thought. What timeless tranquillity was held between the hedgerows of Irish fields. It was familiar and new at the same time. We both hushed to it. Had we been gone only two and a half weeks?

Forty minutes later Larry turned the car off the main road and drove into the village past Knockalough Lake. We were back. Deirdre was moments away. Chris leaned forward in her seat.

"Larry, did she miss us or not?"

"Well, now, I'll let Lucy tell you all about her," he said, turning the car into the driveway.

In a flash, Lucy was out to meet us.

"Welcome back, how are you? Come and see your daughter, she's just after getting up."

"How was she, Lucy?" I asked.

"Wonderful. Come on in and see her."

We tiptoed into the kitchen so charged with emotion and expectation that no words can exaggerate how we felt. Sitting in her pram, Deirdre was quietly turning a plastic lid over and over in her hands. She looked very different. I'll never forget it. She turned her little head up at us to see as we came in, then she simply looked down and returned her attention to her red plastic lid.

And that was it. She showed no sign of recognition whatsoever. To cover it, Lucy hurried over to her. "She's only just got up. I woke her so she'd be awake when you got here. Deirdre, here's Mammy and Daddy. Here's Mammy and Daddy home again." But even as she picked up the baby and turned her to us, our hearts sank and a sickening kind of loss and guilt washed over us. There we were, mother, father, and child, as distant as strangers once again. There were tears in Chris's eyes as she sat down with our baby in her lap. "Hello, Deirdre," she said, but the baby just looked through her. Lucy held Deirdre up for me to take her, but I couldn't. "Put her down for a while by herself and maybe she'll get used to us," I said. "She will, of course," said Lucy, gaily. "Come on—we'll have the breakfast and you tell us all about your trip."

There was a hearty meal of rashers and sausages and eggs and toast, and strong tea. There were warm welcomes from Lucy and Larry's children, Mark, Evan, Pamela, and Michael, as each awoke and came in for breakfast. But for Chris and me there was only an inexpressible aching. We were like people underwater, submerged in a wave of grief and unable to surface. There, in Blakes' kitchen that morning, we had reencountered all the pain of our childlessness. This little baby beside us in the borrowed pram was not even ours yet. It is almost impossible to tell how truly wounded we felt. For foolish as it might seem for us to have even imagined there would be any reaction on Deirdre's part—she was only six months old—we could not help but feel it was in some way a judgment of our own inadequacy as adoptive parents. When Deirdre looked through or beyond us that morning we felt we had lost the bond we had so patiently, delicately wrought between us. Did she not *know*? Did she not recognize we loved her more than anything? Madly?

By midmorning we drove from the village back to Kiltumper. Deirdre was to nap at Lucy's and be brought up to the cottage in the afternoon when the fires were lit and the bags unpacked. The gray light of morning had now turned to sheets of rain, and gazing through the windscreen wipers at our sheltering herd on the hill fields of Tumper, we knew again the desolate feeling of the place, the sense of everything being shut down. We were closed in with ourselves and the rain. Silently, we each tried to push the thought of Deirdre's return to the cottage to a corner of our minds. And yet, the fear was all the time there: what if when Lucy brought her to us, Deirdre cried out for Lucy or clung to her?

Martin Murray was at the cottage to greet us. He had a blazing turf fire set in the Stanley range. But even as he shook our hands and welcomed us back, the cold of the place struck us like a blow. When the three of us sat down in the kitchen together to hear how the cows, the hens, the new turkeys, and Max the cat had all survived our absence, Chris and I kept our coats on. The rain streamed down the kitchen window.

125

Hours later, bags unpacked and rain still falling, the two of us sat alone in the cottage waiting for Deirdre. On the kitchen table were the few presents we had brought her from America, including a miniature wooden horse with the words *Baby's First Christmas* written upon it in gold. I wonder now, in writing this, if we were not the most foolish parents ever, to have felt so grieved that day. We had, of course, nothing to measure against, but with the supersensitivity of adoptive parents we imagined that a child ought to know and react to its father and mother instantly. In the stillness of that first rainy afternoon back in Kiltumper I felt all the selfishness of a lovesick boy wracked with jealousy. Did she not feel how our hearts had leapt when we walked into Blakes' that morning and saw her sitting there? Did she not realize that more than six thousand miles from Clare we had carried the little album of her photographs like a treasure, loving her halfway across the world? Did she not *know*?

At three o'clock Lucy brought her up to Kiltumper.

"There now," she said, carrying her in, "home again, home again. Where's Mammy, where's Daddy?"

Put in her playpen in the center of the kitchen, Deirdre sat impassively with her few toys. She seemed not to notice us, not to care in the slightest that we were right there beside her.

When Lucy left, the three of us sat there nervous as strangers. All we have to do, I was thinking, is let her know how much we love her, and let her know again and again and again. The bonding, the loving, must begin all over again.

That night Deirdre woke in the dark and cried until we came running.

For the next week or so it was all new to us once again. We felt the cold inside our clothes and shook ourselves to get back into routine. Had our very blood changed? For a time it almost seemed as if it had, and I looked at my sweaters in the hot press (the closet) as if maybe they had thinned out since last winter. Clear skies sailed over Ireland and frosty mornings of absolute stillness withered our garden to an end. We dressed Deirdre as if for the North Pole and set her playpen by the fire.

It was like arriving again for the first time. The sharp contrast between west Clare and the world we had just come from seemed to be constantly with us. Comparisons rose continually to our minds and, while visions of the central-heated and carpeted rooms of Westchester flashed before us, we tried to readjust to our routines in even the simplest matters. Had two and a half weeks in America softened us in some way? I feared it had as I shook myself awake in the frozen, pitch-black mornings to hurry out to the haybarn, fill a bag of turf, bring it in with a few dry ash branches, and light a fire in the kitchen before Deirdre stirred.

The winter routine of the farm needed our attention now. The seven calves had to be weaned immediately from the cows and readied for sale; the cows had to be moved to new grazing until we would begin to feed them hay across the wall; and the turkeys' rations had to be increased— "and prepared with boiled water," Chris insisted, smiling at me sweetly. "They prefer it that way."

Turkey fattening. As the weather turned crisp and cold, steaming bowls of meal were brought from the kitchen to the cabin three times a day. Turkey hotel, I called it, watching them gobble the food while I tried to gauge their weight. Were they light for this time of year? Were they feeling the sudden cold in the air? Fresh water was laid on for them twice daily, and several forkfuls of dry hay litter spread out over the slated floor. There were five weeks to Christmas and no comfort was to be spared. When Chris or I carried Deirdre out to the cabin to look in on them, the four birds would flutter and fan their feathers for her like queens in the pride of their majesty. She pointed excitedly at them and they flew up into the air in a great showy fuss. "Aren't they lovely, Deirdre?" Chris would say. "Turkeys, see the turkeys."

Turkeys, don't bang your wings off the cabin walls, I would think, standing next to them. Don't fly too hard, turkeys, don't bruise your meat.

Into the two main cabins across from turkey hotel we had already brought the cows, the calves, and, of course, the goat. With Peter and Francie there to help we had driven the cows into the lower cabin and hurriedly tied the door, then as quietly as possible ushered the distressed calves into the one above it. Thinking to find their mothers, they rushed into the darkened doorway. By the time they realized there was a six-foot-high wall between them and the cows we had the door locked securely.

It was then the bellowing started. At first it was only the sound of annoyance, the raised roar of a cow whose calf had gone to the wrong side of the fence. Within an hour it was a great angry bellow of nature, an incessant clamorous mooing across the wall, a cry from mother to offspring so pitiful it wrenched your heart to hear it. All night, on and off, the cows kept it up. The calves moaned back and walked in circles around the darkened cabin looking for the way they had come in. They mucked the hay I laid for them and cried out in the morning even before I reached the door with their fodder. In the shed next to them the cows were worse; they were cross and defiant, frisky with cabin fever. They snorted when I came in to them. Loops of spittle drooled from their mouths, and to our hopelessly inexperienced eyes, they seemed to look and cry incredibly sadly. Chris and I had special reason of course to feel this so deeply, for, like the plight the year before of Bridget, the Simmental cow who hadn't come into calf and had to be sold, it was something on the farm that seemed so close to our own emotions. It was the kind of thing that brought us swiftly, immediately back to the ways of Kiltumper. Such things were our life here.

When at last the calves were sold and taken away, we let the cows out into the thick aftergrass of the big meadow and watched from the ditch as they galloped forlornly round and round the field looking for their calves.

Thinking about motherhood today. It's not easy being a mother. On the one hand I don't feel like a mother at all. But on the other hand there is this baby beside me— sometimes smiling, sometimes crying, and sometimes just there looking at me (I don't know if she's seeing me or not)—and I am playing the mother. I got to wondering exactly what does "mother" mean anyway. I went to the dictionary and discovered that the first definition is "a female that has borne an offspring." I was afraid of that and a little hurt. But the second definition is "a female who has adopted a child or otherwise established a maternal relationship with another person." Well, that's us. That's me and Deirdre. Only she doesn't know it yet. I wonder what she thinks, or feels, about me. I wonder if a baby born to its mother knows its mother intuitively. I imagine it does and that there is a bond from birth which continues to grow day by day, so that by three months baby and mother *know* one another. With me and Deirdre it's different. That bonding that one hears so much about didn't get a chance to get going until she came to us at ten weeks. And then it broke when we went to America in October and the bonding had to begin all over again. It's so hard, especially not knowing if she will be ours for keeps. We've had her for five months. In another month, we become eligible to adopt her legally. If her biological mother signs her final consent to the adoption agency, then the paperwork can begin. Deirdre's biological mother can still change her mind up until the very minute the adoption order is made, but it's less likely once she signs her final consent. I wonder, will Deirdre know, then? And will I feel more like a "mother." This limbo isn't easy.

To live in a small rural village in the west of Ireland year in, year out, is to know at first hand every shade of the feeling of community. In two and a half years in Kiltumper, of the many things that had changed in our world since dismantling one life in New York and establishing another in Clare, it was this spirit of community that seemed the most salient difference in the quality of our lives. Although now we were certainly living in a place with far fewer people, we were in fact living far more closely to them. We knew who was sick and with what, we knew who had died and what time was his funeral, who was getting married, what babies were born. We knew the people in the village on Sundays, we knew all those who walked in to Mass along our roads, which ones wanted a lift in the car, and which didn't. We knew the scandals and the gossip, and learned to laugh at them, the tall stories and funny tales that blew up in pubs and kitchens when there was nothing else to do. We knew the half-days and the holy days, the mart and fair days, and pub and post office hours of business. We knew farmlands and farmers, machines and cattle, we knew which tractor was parked on the "fall" of ground for the morning start, whose animals had strayed onto the road in the middle of the night, and whose farm they had landed in. We knew the sights, smells, and sounds of this place now, its characters and whimsies. We knew its priests and shopkeepers and small-business people—Paddy the builder, Mary the hairdresser, Michael the doctor, Tommy the blacksmith—and they knew us.

This may be an obvious point about rural life anywhere, and yet, for Chris and me there is a very deep community feeling in the west of Ireland that we had never experienced anywhere before. It is a way of life bound up in the history and geography of the place, inextricably tangled in the brutal poverty of the land, in the harsh irrational weathers that sweep in off the Atlantic, and in the emigration of the young. It is men and women on neighboring farms sharing the same struggle year after year without the slightest hope of wealth. It is a feeling unspoken and, like the sheer beauty of the land all around them, largely unacknowledged. And yet, it is here, a spirit of place and community informing every day. For me, this sense of place and the *belonging* of people to it has been something I have deeply longed to rediscover in Ireland. Like many emigrants, I feared to have lost forever the feeling of belonging and imagined my life in America taking place in a series of suburban settings, each one with its shopping mall, cinema complex, and fast-food station amidst a core of other convenient, mass-market consumer pit stops, one only slightly different from the next.

In coming back to Ireland, Chris and I had hoped to find just this sense of community that we have discovered in

131

the West. In our first year in Kiltumper, the marvelous generosity and openheartedness of our immediate neighbors had begun the process. We had been helped with everything. The Kilmihil Drama Group had also been part of it and a way for both of us to contribute something to the community. There had been Chris's exercise classes in the community center, and a large colorful mural of frogs and birds for the Community Playschool room. One evening Father Leenane, the curate of St. Michael's, had sat for tea in the kitchen and asked Chris's advice on a color scheme for the village hall. And, as she was handy with the paints, would she ever be able to paint a few EXIT and PUSH BAR TO OPEN signs on the doors of the community center? And now, on a still November evening, a whole new dimension was revealed when Larry sat in the kitchen and asked me would I like to take a few teaching hours at the school?

The Kilmihil Vocational School, situated on the road just outside the village, is one of the best schools I have seen in the west of Ireland. A bright new extension had been added to the old building, and the school now includes a full gymnasium, assembly area, metalwork and woodwork rooms, as well as additional classrooms. In all, there are about three hundred students enrolled, studying until their final exams, to obtain the Leaving Certificate at age seventeen. As their principal, Larry knows every one of them. A short man with silver hair and lively blue eyes, his personality is everywhere in the school. It is in the neatness and brightness, the openness and freedom of the place.

I happily consented to teach there.

It was agreed that I would teach for three days a week for the period of one year. Although I had a master's degree in English, because I did not have an education diploma nor was I a member of the Teacher's Union of

Ireland, I would not actually be teaching the curriculum. So I would have no course books or standards or requirements to satisfy. Instead, we decided that I would do my best to instruct the students of the Kilmihil Vocational School in the arts of drama and writing. I thought myself fortunate in stumbling upon an opportunity to give my energy and enthusiasm to a very deserving cause.

"Well, as far as I'm concerned, anything that we can do to help them with writing, the writing of stories, the writing of letters, anything, it will all help them, Niall," said Larry enthusiastically, still sitting on our settee beside the turf-fired stove.

"You could do a play with them," Chris suggested.

"Well now I'll tell you this," cut in Larry firmly, "to be able to go up on stage, lads, is a very important thing for anyone. I think so anyway, don't you, Chris? Sure, it's great for confidence in speaking and everything."

"You could use a tape recorder and set up a little weekly radio show," Chris piped in again.

"And lads, you know, I have a brand-new video camera down there, just waiting for somebody to use it."

"That's it, you could make a film!!!"

It was to be a giddy night of ideas. A second pot of tea and of coffee was made, and one man's vision of the near-limitless possibilities for his school spun a web of excitement around the three of us. I was dizzy with it and marveled at both Larry's openness to such a scheme and his confidence in me. After all, the school, like the church, was at the heart of the community. Could I do it?

"Whatever they get out of it, if only one pupil learns to love plays or stories, haven't we achieved something?" Larry reassured me.

I agreed. A huge moon hung like a beacon beyond the window and I felt like somebody present at the launching of a bright new ship sailing forth to discover a brave new

133

world. But it was happening here, in a quiet little place in the heart of a rural countryside, where a school principal with vision could draw to his school those people in the neighborhood who had something to offer. Here, in action, was the very spirit of community.

A week later, however, the inspiration had cooled. I stood for the first time in a classroom before thirty boys and girls with expectant faces. I had a few notes and possible project plans written out on sheets of paper. When the students' whispering finally stopped my heart was battering in my chest. As I laid out my papers my foot knocked against the teacher's chair and a titter rippled through the room. I looked up to dead silence.

"Listen, I'm not a teacher," I said, "I'm not going to give you homework and I'm not going to follow your English book. What I want to do is get some of you on stage, and others to write jokes and stories for them . . ."

From the front row a boy with full red cheeks and a mischievous smile cut in:

"Then you might as well be sitting while you're standing, sir," he said, and paused. Then again: "*That's* a joke, sir, you might as well be sitting while you're standing, do you get it?"

And with that, the entire class roared with laughter.

I never did get it. And I found it was a very hard job indeed to teach a class of teenagers with neither schoolbooks nor lesson plans to fall back on.

On the clear silver-frosted nights of November, the very air of evening sparkled with crispness. Gathering hurried armfuls of turf from the haybarn, I felt the shimmering cold of the stars themselves in the night sky. So little is ever said of the skies of Ireland, and yet between the majestic cloudscapes—bruised blue-gray thunderheads, mists and fogs of every variety, scudding lighter-than-light fluffballs, strands and veils and sweeps and sprawls of cloud—and the moony, starry night skies over bog and mountain, it is so much a part of landscape.

Under November's fabulous skies, then, infinitely starred, we slipped from the house (with Deirdre asleep in her cot and Pamela baby-sitting) to attend final rehearsals of the Kilmihil Drama Group's latest production. This time, we thought, we had outdone ourselves. After the grand successes of last year, having taken first place with *The Man Who Wouldn't Go to Heaven* in almost every festival we attended, and reaching the All-Ireland Finals for the first time in the drama group's recent history, we knew that this year much was expected of us. It went without saying that, as our last two productions had been successful and somewhat wild comedies, the little bunch of people whom we grandly called our audience were certainly expecting something just as funny, if not funnier, this year.

Even in midsummer, long before the drama season was due to start up again in September, there had been a few inquiries in the village.

"I suppose ye'll have a play ready for Doonbeg again this year?"

"We will."

"What'll it be at all? That one ye did last year was very funny altogether. I'd like to see that one again, so I would."

"Well, we'll have something just as good for you this year, I hope."

"Ye beat everyone with that play last year, didn't ye?"

"Yes."

"Ye beat Ennis and Shannon and Kilrush, the whole lot of 'em?"

"Yes."

"Well, jeekers, there was some funny stuff in that play so

there was. Weren't you the Nun in that one, Crissie? Oh, that was funny, that was . . ."

And on it went. So little by little, as the summer faded and the drama season drew on, the choice of this year's one-act play seemed even more difficult.

"Only a year ago," Chris had said to me one evening as we read and rejected old one-act Irish plays by the dozen, "we were delighted to have come in in third place in Doonbeg. Now look at us."

It was true. Success brought its own drawbacks. For a time we could find no suitable play to propose. Sipping tea at the kitchen table and gazing out over Hayes' Hill, Chris remarked, quite slowly and deliberately, "One of the funniest plays I ever saw was a play by Woody Allen called *God*."

Six weeks later, we were stealing from the cottage into the frosty nights of November to attend final rehearsals of *God*. There was something highly risky and dangerous about the whole business now. We knew that. For here was a one act play by a very brilliant person, attempting, in fifty pages or so, to produce sheer chaos on stage, and to produce it in a very, very funny manner indeed. The play defies summarization, but perhaps it is enough to say that it begins with two Greeks on stage, Diabetes and Hepatitis, one a writer, one an actor. They are hastily trying to find a suitable ending for their play. As they ponder the philosophical and creative problems of all endings, of life and death, Hepatitis asks the audience if anyone out there studied philosophy. A girl, Doris Levine, stands up. And with that, the chaos begins. After Doris arrives on the stage to join the Greeks, anything can happen. And does. There are sudden guest appearances by Blanche DuBois and Groucho Marx; Woody Allen himself calls up on the phone to know how they plan to end the play. There is a God machine, a Greek chorus, a Greek inventor with the hots for Doris, a horde of slaves, a writer, written in by the Writer, two American tourists, a doctor, a woman who was stabbed on the subway, a King from the William Morris agency, a guard, a man in the audience who shoots himself from boredom, and a prompter who occasionally steps out from behind the curtain to speak the lines. There is also a chorus from *The Sound of Music*, a wind machine, a Greek palace, a squirting camera, a hand buzzer, several folding daggers, several nonfolding daggers, a roast beef sandwich, and a one-word message for the King.

With all this then, how could we fail?

Or, more truly perhaps, with all this, how could we possibly manage?

Six weeks into our "season," license fees had been paid, permission had been granted, and in the main assembly area of the Vocational School the big cast gathered three times a week to go over their lines. Everybody was there: Lucy, Tessie, Gerry, Martin, Martin, and Martin, Michael, Rita, Siobhan, Fiona, Brian, Noel, Colm, Doctor Harty as the Doctor, and fourteen-year-old Mark Blake as God. Liz Finucane would make the Greek togas, prompt, and play the Prompter. Her husband, Gerry, along with Larry was building the God machine. As with the previous two years, Chris and I would codirect, and Chris would have the say on design and sets. It was all hectic and exciting. As the weeks went by, you could feel the quickened pulse of a play coming together. Larry wheeled out the converted baby pram and said, "There's the basics of your God machine now." Gerry Harty arrived with the feather boa for Blanche DuBois, Brian Cotter's hand buzzer, or one of the folding daggers. Liz produced the first of the Greek togas and Michael Mescall slipped out to the Gents to try it on. He reappeared in his stocking feet and we all started laughing.

There seemed a thousand things that needed seeing

to—a telephone to receive Woody Allen's call, a tape recorder to play the mimicked Woody Allen dialogue that Chris's cousin Vincent Casey had sent specially from America along with the opening music by the Marx Brothers to set the scene, a child's plastic doctor set for the Doctor to use when he tries to resuscitate God, the Almighty's own thunderbolts, the Queen's crown (with poetic license we changed the King to a Queen and the male playwright to a female author), the stabbed woman's false chest, and a half-dozen pairs of Greek sandals. Everything was listed and searched for, and in the final countdown to the production in Doonbeg the infectious excitement of theater was something you could touch in the air. It was this I loved the most, the feeling I got in the last weeks of a play, when everyone involved seemed intent on the same thing. There was so much team spirit about it all, the men and women of the Kilmihil Drama Group who by day worked in their kitchens, farms, schoolrooms, and offices, and by night became actors, stage managers, lighting men, designers. It was like night magic in November, and as rehearsals broke up and the cast went to their cars in the moonlight, or in the rain, the streets home glittered with dreams.

In the clearer light of day there'd be anxious telephone calls: What do you think about my accent? Or, how do I look in that outfit? Or, how should I say that? Or, when exactly do I stab him?

Needless to say, the humor and language of Woody Allen are foreign to west Clare. We knew this when the play was chosen, and a large part of the risk involved in putting it on was bound up with one simple question: *Would they laugh?* For the purposes of our performances, and yet in keeping with the mood and spirit of the original, a few changes had necessarily been made to the text. Doris Levine was no longer a Jewish girl from Long Island, but now came all the way from Cork City. The woman on the subway was not reading the New York *Post* but London's *Daily Mirror*, and spoke with a thick Belfast accent. The Queen was from Dublin. Other concessions to the audience involved the bleeping of a few words here and there. In the original text when Lorenzo Miller (who became Lorenza) tells Doris she's not real, Doris replies firmly: "I am real, what's more I have orgasms." This was generally agreed to be a bit risky, and so in the Kilmihil Drama Group's production, Gerry Harty would simply say: "I am real, what's more I . . .," wriggling her body and raising her eyebrows to show the audience what she meant. None of the meaning was lost, and in fact, it seemed a testament to how well drawn the characters and situation were. It mattered not a bit that our God was fourteen years old, that our *deus ex machina* was a battered pram, or that instead of a full-blown Greek chorus we were using a six-by-four foot board upon which Chris had painted a number of Greek figures, which bore the heading, "A BUNCH OF GREEKS." It would all work just the same.

Or so it seemed to us during the last week of rehearsal. On Thursday we saw the advertisement for the West Clare Drama Festival in Doonbeg in the *Clare Champion*. There on the final night was *God* by Woody Allen, and as Chris and I went down to the village the following day there were a few inquiries.

"What is it called again?"

"*God*," I said. That drew a smile right away.

"Oh, sort of the same thing as last year, is it? *God*, sort of a follow-up to *The Man Who Wouldn't Go to Heaven?* Is it by the same fellow?"

"No, it's by Woody Allen," I said. This made no effect. "Well sure that play ye had last year was very funny."

On Friday night there was a final rehearsal in the

school. Timing is everything in comedy, and that night between Michael as Hepatitis crawling across the stage in his toga to whisper "Get off, you're ruining my play," Martin tickling Queen Lucy with the false dagger, and Mark's appearance as God (DIABETES: God is dead. DOCTOR: Does He have any insurance?), we almost fell over with laughter. Later as I drove Pamela back home from baby-sitting she asked me: "Is the play funny?" "Hilarious," I said, "we'll have them laughing for a week."

Sunday night, showtime. Larry, Gerry Finucane, Chris, and I went early to Doonbeg. A sleepy little place by the sea on a Sunday afternoon in November, it was hard to imagine that later that evening the village hall would be thronged with men, women, and children eager to see plays. For the one-act festival there were three productions each night with a ten-minute changeover allowed, and at the end of each evening the adjudicator—usually someone who had been involved in theater professionally in one capacity or another—stepped to the stage and read out his or her comments on what the audience had seen. It was not uncommon for adjudicators to be highly laudatory, or highly critical. The actors often sat in the wings still in costume, like so many accused waiting to hear sentence. On Sunday, the final night, there was an added tension, for, besides the normal adjudication, there were the overall awards for Best Play, Best Producer, Best Actor, Best Actress, and so on.

As we arrived at the hall that Sunday, we handed over last year's silver cup to Mort, one of the leading figures in the Amateur Drama Council and the tireless Doonbeg festival organizer. "I suppose we'll be giving this back to you later this evening," he said, taking it from me.

"Please *God*," I said, with only the slightest trace of a smile.

By eight that evening the long narrow Doonbeg hall was packed. Mort had reappeared in a tuxedo and hovered up and down the aisles finding last-minute seating and checking on the readiness of the actors. Corofin Drama Group were first on, and until they took to the stage we had to keep out of the dressing rooms. I watched them set their stage and fiddled with the program. After a while, another tuxedoed figure took his place at the little lit table at the back of the hall. The adjudicator was in position. Suddenly Mort was in front of the curtain and the houselights had gone down. "Good evening again, ladies and gentlemen, and welcome to the final night of this year's one-act drama festival . . ."

In a flash we were all in the dressing room with the makeup box out and tissues flying. Michael and Martin put on their togas, Rita and Brian strolled about in their colorful American tourist outfits, Tessie and Lucy, first ready, were going over their lines in a low hum in the corner. From outside we heard the audience laughing loudly at the Corofin play. Then a round of applause. Then more laughter. "They seem to be enjoying that one, Niall," said Gerry Harty, a little anxiously. "Don't worry about them," I said, like an impresario. "They haven't seen *God*."

Moments later, we heard a thunderous round of applause, as the Corofin Players took their bow and came clambering down the stairs into the dressing room. Immediately Larry, Chris, and Gerry Finucane went up to ready the stage. I stayed with the actors. There were last-minute worries fluttering everywhere: shouldn't Doris take her seat in the audience now? Where was Noel sitting and what if his gun didn't go off? Niall, the paint on the BUNCH OF GREEKS is still wet, look!

At once Mort reappeared at the stage door: "Everybody ready?" There was a last-minute check, and then Gerry Finucane left to go down to the lighting board. Chris and I took up our positions in the wings and the houselights went down. There was a pause, that hushed expectant moment into which it seemed all the preparation of the past weeks was crammed. Then, over the air rose the quick light music of the Marx Brothers, and to its beat Larry pulled open the curtain.

What happened after that was a kind of actor's nightmare. Peering from the wings I saw Michael strike the pose of the Thinker and Martin emerge from inside the Actor's Chest. I heard the first lines go eerily out over the heads of the packed audience. There was absolutely no response. Not a sound, not a titter of laughter. Doris came from her seat and marched up onto the stage, Woody Allen called on the phone, Blanche DuBois sashayed in and draped herself across Hepatitis' lap, and still there was barely a laugh. It was only when Noel, on cue, stood up in the audience and said: "I'm leaving. When I go to see a play I expect to see something with a beginning, a middle, and an end, instead of this bullshit!" that a sudden round of applause rang out. Still, on we went with it, the play dying on its feet even as the actors tried harder and harder. God appeared, and died. And then the curtain closed to the Marx Brothers music once again.

At that moment, it didn't strike any of us that the chemistry on the night had just gone wrong. At that moment there was only a dazed feeling of disappointed amazement. There was no final bow, we had flopped.

We still came in third and were praised for tackling such a difficult piece. Two nights later we packed the whole show into Gerry Finucane's van and performed *God* at the Limerick Drama Festival, coming second there, and third at the festival in Pallas Green three nights later. Finally, after it was all over, we treated ourselves to a postproduction slap-up meal at Sean Fitz's down in the village. We had flopped at Doonbeg, but we'd carried on. We were the Kilmihil Drama Group.

This afternoon as the sky was darkening to evening I met Francie as I was cycling home from the village. I came upon him by the edge of a drain on the side of the road. Francie called it a river. He had a bucket and was standing alone. I was quite interested in what he was doing there in the closing darkness of a cold afternoon. With all the innocence of childhood, he told me, "I'm trying to catch an eel." "An eel!" I exclaimed. "You're kidding," I added. "No, Crissie" he said, "I'm going to catch an eel." I persisted in my disbelief, wondering if he might not be trying to joke with me. So I played along, wink wink, nudge nudge, and all that. But Francie was earnest. I finally asked him what did he want this eel for and, more important, who told him he might find one there in the open drain. After all, didn't he know that the water was only flowing there as it drained from the land above it. It wasn't a river or a stream, or even a brook. Yes, he knew that, he said. And it was Mary who told him to come here and it was Bridey who told him to catch an eel, because "You know what, Crissie, an eel has very little blood." This was certainly an education for me. He continued, "And when I catch him, I'm going to chop off his head and bring him home to Mammy. Because Crissie, if you smear the blood on warts, the warts go away!"

Shades of Tom Sawyer.

CHAPTER EIGHT

It was a pitch-black night in late November. Leafless trees stood absolutely still and the dark shapes of cattle moved softly in the wet fields. It was the kind of midwinter night in Kiltumper that made you feel closed into the hushed solitary heart of the world. The kind of night that wrapped itself around you, made the whole townland snug within itself, and breathed out through the darkness the enormous peace of living here. The distant cottages flickered like candles miles away. Turf smoke rose and faded into the breezeless dark and from little drains and rivulets the sound of water ran through the night air. It was still and quiet and cool and lovely. It was Thanksgiving night and Chris and I went walking slowly through the dark to the light at Tom and Mary Brogan's.

Tom and Mary had been married fifty years, and tonight in Kiltumper they were having mass in their house to celebrate. As we reached the bend in the road we saw their house lights shine out across the fields. The whole Brogan family, many traveling from England, would be gathered in the home place.

As we reached the door Mary Brogan was there to meet us.

"You're welcome, Crissie; you're welcome, Niall," she said, shaking our hands warmly and showing us into the bright parlor where already some of our neighbors were gathered. Tom came up to us, moving across the room in his blue suit, leaning a little on his walking-stick. He stretched out a hand of welcome and smiled.

"Happy anniversary, Tom," said Chris.

"Thank you, Crissie," he said, with a little bow of his head.

"Tom," I asked him, when we had sat down, "do you remember at all the day of your wedding?"

"I do," he said brightly. "It was a lovely day. I remember everything about it. There were no cars around in those days, of course—it was all horses and carts. I remember going down to the church, not the new church now, but down by the graveyard where the old church used to be. And I remember the priest coming out on the altar and Mary coming in the door." He paused a moment as if to revisit the moment. There in the parlor, he seemed to walk entranced through his wedding day a half a century ago, and then his eyes smiled and lifted to where Mary was bringing Father Leenane in the door.

For the rest of that evening in Brogans' that moment held me. I sat quietly with Chris and joined with everyone in the celebratory mass, the soft murmurings of the prayers of thanks floating out from the house of fifty years of marriage, drifting across the motionless fields of darkened Kiltumper and rising into the black night of heaven. I sat and said the prayers and looked at Chris. I thought of what coming here had meant to us. *How is it all going, then?* I thought of the sacrifices and the rewards, the bad days and the good days, the rainy garden and summer in the meadow. In my mind's eye I saw Tom's smile again, and thought to myself: what a solid little world is held in a cottage and what marvelous love can live within it. I reached to touch Chris's hand. Music was starting, teapots were circling the room as laughter bubbled into the air. Outside nothing was moving for miles around. It was Thanksgiving night.

Thanksgiving in Kiltumper once again. A gray, dull day, not crisp like at home at this time of year. With no *Yanks* about to celebrate with me, Thanksgiving in Ireland passes with a dull ache like just another Thursday. Here, we must generate for ourselves a Thanksgiving spirit and acknowledge, by ourselves, everything we are grateful for. At distant tables, family and friends in America are passing the cranberry sauce and pumpkin pie. I'd give anything right now for a pumpkin pie, even a store-bought frozen pie. So, mustering a festive mood and trying to quell my homesickness, I set about making "the Christmas Cake."

A pound of raisins, a pound of currants, mixed peel, and chopped cherries. Twelve ounces of margarine, ground almonds, and several liberal tablespoons of cinnamon, nutmeg, and ground cloves. Twelve ounces of brown sugar, seven free-range eggs, and nearly a pound of flour. The grated rind of an orange and two lemons, and three healthy capfuls of Irish whiskey for preservation! Creamed together the traditional way and baked slowly for five hours, Grandma Kitty's Irish fruitcake is ready to be wrapped in aluminum and safely stored in the hot press until Christmas.

I remember when I was a child we used to spend some of the Thanksgiving holiday at Grandma Kitty's in Elmhurst, Queens. The treat we all longed for after dinner was her special fruitcake. I always thought it was her secret recipe and no one else in the whole world knew how to make it. Now I know that every good Irish wife and mother knows how to make Grandma Kitty's fruitcake. So here I was, many years after my first bite of an Irish Christmas Cake, baking my own "from scratch" and relishing every crumb and currant as if it were Grandma's own.

Winter was stealing in upon us once more. We woke to feel the cold inside the cottage and hurried to pull on double-jumpers, or sweaters, and light the morning fire. Only Deirdre awoke to warmth. We didn't carry her into the kitchen for breakfast until the first glowing of the turf. This probably wasn't necessary; thousands of Irish children woke in cottages like this one and toddled barefoot into the kitchen. And yet, on mornings when frost whitened the fields outside, the air inside our stone walls froze ears, feet, and the tips of noses. At Chris's insistence we left Deirdre's heater on all night.

Outside there was all around us the emptiness of early December, clear, windless, and still. The world seemed suspended in awaiting the advent of Christmas. Mornings after breakfast we tossed handfuls of stale breadcrumbs across the frozen potato ridges to keep the birds from picking the berries off the holly tree. Out about the cabins, I banged my feet in my Wellingtons to keep warm, and carried bag upon bag of turf into the kitchen. I could see our turf rick diminishing quickly and feel the chill threat of such cold words as January, February, and March. Surely we had enough fuel? The cows in the late grass of the back meadow smelled hay on the air, and every morning came charging to the wall, their great watery eyes watching me move a bale of hay. They nosed along the stone walls, waiting. I waited too, each day delaying the beginning of winter feeding, each day counting the number of bales against the days until spring. Surely we had enough fodder? I brought in turf and put out no hay, and heard the cows behind me bellow and press a little more forcibly against the single strand of wire that kept them from the haybarn.

The basic question is: What are teething pains? Today is the sixth of December, 1987, and Deirdre got her first tooth! So far so good. No pain. No sleepless nights. And one little white tootheen.

With Deirdre hatted, coated, and wrapped in a kind of pink feather-down envelope that Chris's mother had sent from America, we went walking up the hills of Tumper, crossing the stone walls, passing the baby between us and stopping for her to peep out as a startled pheasant clattered into the air. We climbed to the distant view of Kerry across the fields and paused by the mound of Tumper's Grave, where, according to legend, the giant himself is buried. Here, centuries of Chris's ancestors had stood, looking west to the Atlantic, east to Limerick, or south to the Shannon. Here, we held Deirdre between us, the newest, latest viewer of this sweep of hilly, rocky, west Clare land that had become her home. Below, we pointed out to her the rising smoke of our cottage through the trees, the whitened necklace of little stone walls that fringed the fields, the motionless figures of the cows, and the blessed well over by Sean's bounds. We pointed them all out and carried her on with us over the hilltop, walking where the hare and fox trails crisscrossed the spongy brown surface of the bog. In by the sally trees and across the drain; this is the way to the bog, Deirdre, I said to her, making Chris laugh out loud. See where the heather will bloom and fleck the place with sprigs of purple in the summer, see where the cuckooflower will grow for your birthday.

Passing the baby between us, we crossed on into the forestry, moving between the thicket of the trees and smelling the clean sharp smell of spruce on the frosty air. Here was a little Christmas spirit on the top of Tumper, man, woman, and child going slowly, dreamlike, through the still, becalmed forest of December. We made our way carefully, stumbling a little between the uneven, ridged plantings, squelching and puddling where the thin frost crunched underfoot and our boots became bog-seeped and muddied.

"See the Christmas trees, Deirdre," said Chris, pulling the covering down from around the baby's face and letting her lovely blue eyes peer out. She gazed for a moment at the trees, and in her gaze I could actually see the wonder of what it looked like for her. I could feel the newness of all this, and the very great ancientness of it, too. Thousand of years earlier giant oak trees had stood here in the very place where the young forest of spruce was now growing. We said not a word, hearing our breaths fade upon the air.

Captain Mac was due at two. At four he had a pig to kill in Cooraclare, and more turkeys back in the townland of Leitrim after that. This was his busy season and as arranged Lucy and Tessie would bring him from the village up to Kiltumper. Waiting, I paced about in the yard. At the slightest sound of my footsteps on the gravel, there came a frantic rush of cries through the locked door of turkey hotel. Deliberately then, I walked instead up by the long grass about the haybarn, easing my conscience by telling myself that our four nameless birds had, after all, enjoyed the fullest menu three times daily for months. This, I knew, was the kind of specious reasoning that city people in the country allowed themselves, not being quite hardened either to the realities of farm life, or to the idea of slaughter. Yet, it was with just this kind of internal argument that I found myself preoccupied as I waited for the Captain. Chickens we could more or less kill ourselves now, but two of these turkeys were Christmas gifts for Lucy and Tessie, and faced with the much greater size and strength of the birds, I told myself it would be foolish to attempt them alone. What if I didn't quite kill them? What if they flew from my grasp, their heads half-strangled and their eyes crazy with life? No. Better to book the Captain. He was our village expert and had seen the deaths of more animals than he cared to remember. From our first months in Kilmihil we had seen him around the village: a low-sized middle-aged man of strong build, with long, bushy sideburns that curl around his cheeks, wearing a hat and riding a big black bicycle. There was nothing about animals he didn't know, he had had years of experience of every kind of farm incident. He knew at first hand all the interior secrecies of cows, horses, pigs, geese, ducks, hens, and other animals, he knew their workings and their ways, and, in contrast to the vastness of our inexperience and ignorance, he was country-wise and Clare cute. He was the best man for the job.

At ten past two he stepped from Tessie's car, and immediately cocked his ear to the desperate sounds of the birds in the cabin below.

"You've 'em locked in tight?" he asked with a glint in his eye, smiling at me from beneath his green felt hat. "How many have you?"

"Four," I told him, not exactly sure if this was a lot or a little.

There was a momentary pause as Chris came out and the three of us stood around while the Captain readied himself. He had his killing coat, a brownish garment with faded blood and other stains of vaguer origin, tied in a neat bundle with a piece of cord. Putting it on, he took off his hat for a moment.

"You've always had a hat, Captain," Tessie remarked.

"I've had a hat on my head for these past forty years. They said I'd be bald at thirty, and I'm sixty-one." He showed us his fine head of hair, and popped his hat back on. "Now, young fella, where you going to kill these turkeys?"

Tessie got back into her car. "I'll be back in a minute," she said, and drove hurriedly away.

"You don't need me, right?" said Chris. "I'll be in the

kitchen. Okay?" And she and Lucy smartly vanished into the kitchen where a low turf fire burned on the open hearth floor.

"Well, they disappeared quickly," I said, leading the Captain to the small cabin next to turkey hotel, "We can pluck them in here," I added, pointing to a large wooden box I had set out especially for the feathers.

"Fair enough," he said, and reached out to touch the handle of Chris's short spade lying next to the wall. I stared for a moment; he looked up at me. "Well, get the first one so," he said.

Of course, they heard me coming. Light-headed and wild with hunger, they came at a flutter, all wings and beaks, bunching and pecking angrily at the rotting timber of the cabin door. It was like a mad gobbling flight out of a starving nightmare: I had simply forgotten to feed them for a few days, this time I was surely coming with their food. Their beaks worked on air at the thought of it: a steaming bowl of meal, garden peas and potato skins, warm water, brownbread crumbs and Turkey Fattener. I pulled the double bolts and entered the cabin as loudly as possible without betraying myself to the Captain outside. The birds scattered to the back wall, and in the beam of light from the door, I crouched to catch the first one. Start with the biggest or the smallest? My hand flew out to grab a foot and with a squawk of fright the turkey rose up into the air and away from me. Start with the nearest.

Suddenly I had one. I had her by the feet, I had her upside down, disoriented or dizzy, the blood rushing like deep purple to her brain and the frozen discs of her eyes staring alarmed at the world turned on its head. For a moment I might have let her go, for a moment it might have been enough just to have stood there and held her so like that, the fullness of her, the amazing whiteness of her feathers, the depth to her breast, the span of her wings.

For a moment there in the dim light of the cabin I was stunned by the thing I was about to do. Then, the great racket of the turkeys rising again and the weight of the bird quivering in my grasp, I rushed to the door.

"You got one?" asked the Captain, smiling, whipping a piece of cord about the bird's legs, knotting, double-knotting it, and then taking the live animal in his hands for a moment to weigh it in the air. "A nice-sized turkey, that one," he said, holding it out before him and pulling a few feathers from the base of the neck. "A little less than twenty pounds or so, I'd say."

We moved matter-of-factly in a little huddle from the turkey hotel to the slaughter cabin. The afternoon air was cool and still. The cows in the back meadow had come to the wall and the hens were clucking at their door. "Now," said the Captain, "hold her there a minute, young fella. Right. Now lower the head down a bit so I can get this across it." Holding her by the feet I let her down softly and watched in a kind of mute amazement as he laid the handle of the spade neatly over her head.

"Put your feet either side of that now, that's it, that's it perfectly now," he said, as I pressed a little harder with each of my feet, pinning the bird's head to the ground. "Sure you'll be able to do this one yourself, will you?"

I cannot imagine now what made me say yes. Certainly neither the Captain nor I expected it, and yet there I was blurting it out, tightening my grip on the turkey claws and readying to pull upwards. Within seconds it was happening; I could feel the turkey's neck tighten and stretch as, in a kind of daze, I saw my hands rise higher and higher on my waist. I jerked the bird upwards as I knew I was supposed to do, to kill it instantly, humanely. But nothing seemed to be happening. I heard no sound, the neck seemed to be stretching forever, and then, pop! The head shot off. I staggered back with the turkey, her wings beating madly and blood spattering everywhere. A long string of red stuff dangled from where the head had been, and in my astonishment my eyes could see nothing but that, that dripping jellied vacancy where the head was missing. The head was missing!! As the bird thrashed and fluttered with last life and blood flecked a circle on the gravel all around me, I could hardly believe it. What was I supposed to do? I wanted to put my hand around the neck, close off the hole, stop the blood, find the dead head and stick it back again. But even as such thoughts flashed past me I heard the Captain's voice.

"Give her here, give her here. Run and get a rag, will you?"

At the kitchen door I stopped and saw the blood on my boots. Bending round the door, I called to Chris.

"Can I have a rag, Chris?"

"A rag?"

"Yes."

"What do you want a rag for?"

"The Captain wants it."

"What for?" she asked, innocently enough, putting aside some of Deirdre's clothes and going to the cupboard to get one.

"Well, it's a bit of an emergency, Chris. Could you. . ."

She stopped right where she was and looked at me. I gave up.

"The head's popped off," I said.

"*What?*"

"The turkey's head popped off. It was an accident, I. . ."

"NIALL, THE TURKEY'S HEAD POPPED OFF??"

"Yes," I said, quietly, "we would like a rag to stop the blood."

Speechless, she held out the rag, and sheepishly I took it. It was one of my old socks. At the cabin the Captain had already begun to remedy my disaster. With the flicker of a smile in his eye he took the sock from me and slipped it over the bird's neck, tying it tightly with twine. Then, hanging the turkey by its lifeless claws up on one of the cabin joists, he pulled his hat low on his brow and we both started plucking.

"I think I'd better do the rest of 'em. That lady gave you a bit of a struggle," he said with a chuckle, replaying the scene to himself, and bending into the feather box to bring up the evidence. "You see, you pulled the head clean off her," he giggled, holding it out for me in the palm of his hand.

Niall, Deirdre, and I went to Dublin last weekend for the christening of our godchild, Robert John Williams, Declan and Patricia's second baby. Deirdre slept two of the four hours of the journey, but got sick all over her lovely pink woolen outfit and all over the front of my sweater. Deirdre was lucky; at least I had a change of clothes for her!

Until this weekend, Deirdre has been spending most of her waking hours in a playpen, where she lies on her back or sits, propped up, playing with her toys. She hates to be on her belly and when she rolls from back to front and finds herself on her stomach, she turns back around. Since our cement floor in the kitchen is covered with only a thin layer of linoleum, we hardly ever let her down on it, especially now that it's winter and the floor is very cold. Plus, it's so slippery it's hard for Deirdre to maneuver herself. But Declan and Patricia's house is carpeted and warm and much more inspiring for a seven-and-a-half-month-old baby, as we found out when we laid Deirdre on her belly on the floor beside her cousin, Neil. There, in front of Grandpa Jack and Grandma Philo, she raised herself up with her arms, and tucked her stockinged legs up beneath her, and pushed off! She went forward about an inch and tried it again and again until she looked like a fish out of water flapping her legs and arms in slow transport across the carpet. I think she was, for the first time in her life, happy to be looking down at the world, even if she was only an inch away from it.

With two days to go to Christmas, we decided to seek out the hustle and bustle of shopping streets and lively crowds and take a quick trip to Galway, our favorite city in Ireland. The old blue Peugeot was fueled and oiled, and with Pamela minding Deirdre for the day, we took the Gort road, bringing Thackeray's *Irish Sketch Book* of 1842 along for company. Chris read it aloud as the windscreen wipers slapped at the drizzle.

"'It is the only town in Ireland I have seen where an antiquary can find much subject for study, or a lover of the picturesque an occasion for using his pencil. It is a wild, fierce, and most original old town.'"

"Wild and fierce?" I said.

"Yes, and listen to this:

"'The waters of Lough Corrib, which permeate under the bridges of the town, go rushing and roaring to the sea with a noise and eagerness only known in Galway; and along the banks you see all sorts of strange figures washing all sorts of wonderful rags, with red petticoats and redder shanks standing in the stream. Pigs are in every street, the whole town shrieks with them. There are numbers of idlers on the bridges, thousands in the streets, humming and swarming in and out of dark old ruinous houses; congregated round numberless apple-stalls, nail-stalls, bottle-stalls, pig's-foot stalls; in queer old shops that look to be two centuries old; loitering about warehouses, ruined or not; looking at the washerwomen washing in the river, or at the fish donkeys, or at the potato-stalls, or at a vessel coming into the quay, or at the boats putting out to sea.'"

Chris stopped and looked over at me, as we passed Oranmore and sped on the last mile into the city.

"Sounds pretty wild and fierce to me," she said.

"Yes." I grinned. "Pigs in every street, the whole town *shrieking* with them!"

It wasn't until we were on our way back to Clare that we read further and realized that Thackeray's impressions of the city had been gleaned from the briefest intercourse with it. For as he wrote:

". . .it was pouring with rain, and as English waterproof cloaks are not waterproof in *Ireland,* the traveller who has but one coat must of necessity respect it, and had better stay where he is, unless he prefers to go to bed while he has his clothes dried. . ."

On this basis, of course, the nineteenth-century tourist (with English cloak) would have spent vast chunks of his Irish tour sitting indoors by the fire. As we drove that morning into Eyre Square in the heart of the city, the wetter-than-waterproof Galway rain was nothing more than the softest of sea mists. Parking the car and stepping out into the excited rush of Christmastime, we felt at once the pulse of the city, its *wild, fierce,* and *original* qualities, its strange combination of country fair town and metropolitan city, the gray light and the colorful shopfronts. To the sound of ceili music we headed down the narrow winding path of Shop Street.

To Chris and me it has always seemed that there is something undeniably romantic about Galway City. Everywhere you sense the sea and the mountains about you, sea gulls swoop in the morning square and on a winter's day the air seems tanged with salt. Alleyways and arched passages wind like secrets between old stone buildings, and even the street names seem to conjure images from a more romantic past. Buttermilk, Druid, and Deadman's lanes; the Fishmarket and Flood Street, Spanish Parade and the Spanish Arch. Here, wandering among these places, it is not so difficult to feel the presence of previous centuries—Thackeray's Galway shrieking with pigs, or the cobbled streets through which Christopher Columbus is said to have strode, marching from the quay to hear morning mass at the Church of Saint Nicholas of Myra, patron saint of all travelers by land and sea. Such things have embued Galway with a romance that lingers still, and to walk from the city around Spanish Parade and out by the little quay known as the Claddagh is to move in an atmosphere soaked in history.

All this is part of shopping in Galway. What's more, the streets bustle with lively young and old Galwegians. Galway tweed and Galway wool is everywhere, and small attractive shops selling socks, sweaters, suits, shoes, fishing tackle, vegetables, and books are packed snugly between the pubs. Two days before Christmas, this was just what we needed. We would find something for Santa to bring to Deirdre, and for ourselves, we'd get a visit to Kenny's.

Kenny's Bookshop and Gallery in High Street, Galway,

is one of those places of which a book lover dreams. There, behind an old-fashioned green shopfront are three floors, an attic, and a basement full of books. There is a room for rare books, an antiquarian map and print gallery, and a literature room. There are Irish interest books, travel books, and children's books in Irish, books in foreign languages, and books on religion, law, humanities, medicine, and history. There is a pamphlets and periodicals department, and a very fine art gallery at the back of the shop (or at the front of the shop, depending on where you enter, from High Street or Middle Street). The shop fills the ground floor all the way between the two streets. Here, the Kenny family run a shop for books, restoring them to their place of special honor. There are literally books everywhere, stacked along the winding stairs that take you to the second and third floors, on window ledges, in wicker baskets and corners, in boxes and crates waiting to be unpacked. The walls are festooned with the paintings of contemporary Irish artists. Connemara and the west beckon in a series of extraordinary landscapes, and to open a copy of old Thackeray's nineteenth century *Irish Sketch Book* while surrounded by these paintings is almost to see his coach winding through the rainswept mountains. Here and there, in the various rooms, chairs are left near the shelves. Eye and finger traverse the thousand brown, blue, red, green, and black hardcover volumes of old books on the bookshelves like treasures, and the thought of the winter ahead in a west Clare cottage is suddenly sweetened with the excitement of reading. There is an atmosphere here like that of the city itself. Customers start up a chat with Mrs. Kenny across the counter, the talk is weather or news or books, and a hundred-year-old travelogue of Ireland might be as much in the talk as anything of today. Somebody will come in with an old copy of a favorite book, and one of the Kennys will take it gently, sending it down to their Fine Binding workshop, where it will be bound in soft leather with new end papers, tooled and gilded, and topped with a silken tassel.

That afternoon in Galway, two days before Christmas, Chris and I browsed giddily through Kenny's like children in a toyshop. Before rushing out again into the afternoon air of High Street to shop for Santa, we had chosen a small varied selection of Irish winter reading: the Irish poet Aidan Matthews' first book of short stories, *Adventures in a Bathyscope*; Christopher Nolan's prize-winning *Under the Eye of the Clock*; and two classics of Irish literature, Robin Flower's evocative account of his time among the poets and storytellers of the Great Blasket Island, *The Western Island*, and lastly, an old favorite, a small hardbound copy of John Millington Synge's *The Aran Islands*. For years now, since I had first read it in a Dublin library, I had been meaning to buy it. It was one of those books that seemed to have entered my imagination, touched off something inside of me without my quite realizing it. And, although Chris and I had often spoken of a trip to the Islands since moving to Clare, I had never yet set foot there. Now, I thought, clutching the book as we hurried around the shops of Galway, there was a place that was *wild, fierce, and original*. And, almost like a Christmas present to myself, I knew that this year, after I'd reread Synge's little book, Chris and I would take the boat to Aranmore. Walking in Galway, I pictured those sea-swept islands in the bay, and wondered to myself: whatever would poor Thackeray have made of them?

Lucy arrived with a bagful of mince pies, and taking one of the clean plucked turkeys carefully from where he hung upside down in the cabin, we laid him in the backseat of her car. Socky, as Chris called our headless candidate, was to be held over three more chill days until her brother Sean, my brother Paul, and Chris's cousin, P. J. Brown, arrived in Kiltumper. Surely they wouldn't object to Socky? We'd save the gory tale of his last day until after dessert.

It was Deirdre's first Christmas. Two years previously we had felt deep grief in being childless at Christmastime. It had seemed a specially difficult time of year for us, cut off from all the joy of Santa Claus and Bethlehem. Christmas was a time of children, when childlessness seemed cruelest. But Deirdre had changed all that. In the quiet evenings when she was put to bed, Chris and I sat by the fire in the kitchen. We were like people choked up with emotion, ready to cry at any moment. Our gratitude to the world seemed inexpressible. One moment we were happier than we ever dreamed, sitting there, laughing, and telling over some little thing the baby did that day, a mimicked face, a sound, a gesture, the next we were fretting with all the insecurities and worries first-time adoptive parents—parents on probation still—sometimes know. *Are we doing it right?* Chris would ask, gazing into the glow of the turf fire, and very softly beginning to cry. *Are we doing all right?* Together then in the nighttime, we would sneak across the darkened cottage to Deirdre's bedroom, open the door very, very, very carefully, and stand there and gaze in on her as she slept. What a picture she made, snuggled deeply in covers and almost smiling in her dreams. To see her so made everything right, and the tears coming back to the kitchen were all of joy.

The Christmas tree in the parlor was bedecked with a hundred little wooden ornaments that, each year of our marriage, Chris had collected and dated and hung upon the tree like testaments to our life together. They were among the first things she had packed away to bring from America, and every Christmas in Kiltumper the seven

Downes children had come back along the road to see them all. This year, there were new ones, too. And there, dangling in the front, was the lovely minature white rocking horse with the golden words, *Baby's First Christmas, 1987,* written across it. Every morning of Christmas week, Chris carried Deirdre from her bed through the parlor to gaze at the tree and underneath, at the little gathering of the brightly wrapped presents that had come for her from California, New York, Dublin, and Kilmihil.

All around us we could feel the countryside getting ready. Down in Kilmihil Santa had arrived, and little clusters of children, brought into the village while their parents went about buying "the Christmas," gathered outside the shop windows, gazing with the same gaze that meant Christmas everywhere. While the fields were stilled and frosty, the chill air seemed quickened with excitement. Everywhere houses were being cleaned from top to toe, great fires were being put down in the hearths and ranges, and out along the quiet back roads people were making their Christmas visits—their *cuairds.* There was a real pastoral loveliness to Christmas in the west of Ireland countryside, and this year we felt a keen part of the celebration. Bringing Deirdre in Tessie's borrowed pram, we went around the bumpy road into Upper Kiltumper to visit Dooleys. Since the baby arrived we had been less able to go out *cuairding* to our neighbors in the evenings, and had missed out on a whole range of delights: Pauline's delicious brown scones, Breda's marvelous griddle bread cooked by the open fire, Mary's brownbread and fruitcake, not to mention the innumerable mugs of hearty strong black tea. Now, on the last days before Christmas, we wheeled Deirdre ahead of us and sampled the lot. We sat in Dooleys' kitchen for our "tea" and watched Deirdre playing with Michael and Breda's grown-up daughters, Bernie and Geraldine; we came to the plates of cakes and buns on the table down at Mary's with Joe holding out his hand for Deirdre to grasp. We stopped in with Michael and Pauline, and laughed at all the things Noel and Una and Colette and Evelyn and Karol and Peter and Francie had written to Santa for. We felt a part of it all, bumping the baby back and forth along those roads in Kiltumper, and thinking of all our friends here and the help and welcome they had so generously extended to us since the day we arrived. That, too, was Christmas. Deirdre giggled as we banged over the last pothole home, and at the sound of her laughter our two hens came scampering out the gravel drive to meet the pram.

Christmas Eve, 1987. I've been waiting since we returned from San Francisco last October to dress Deirdre in this little red velvet sleeping suit. Now on Christmas Eve, she's all decked out in her red Santa's helper's outfit and sitting beneath the tree. As we're going up to Dublin to spend Christmas with Niall's parents, Jack and Philo, we decided to open our gifts now. We played our one Christmas tape: Anne Murray's Christmas Carols, turned on the Christmas tree lights, or "fairy" lights as they're called here, and turned off the room light. It wasn't totally romantic, as we had to bring in the bar heater to keep us from freezing since there is no heat in the parlor, but it was wonderful. The tiny white lights of the tree sparkled in Deirdre's eyes as she looked at the Nativity scene we had laid out at the bottom of the tree, at the cow on top of the barn and the gray donkey, at the Three Wise Men with golden gift boxes, at Mary and Joseph and baby Jesus, and at the shepherd boy tending the traveler's camels.

She was very eager to get at the presents under the tree, or rather, to get at the bright and colorful wrapping paper. We gave her her first present: a red teddy bear with a green sweater. She threw it aside and reached out for more. And more followed: three outfits, or "costumes" as Niall calls them; a baby's mug; a little doggie in a bag; a piggy pull-string music toy; two plastic teethers in the shape of a hand and a foot; two duckie sponges; multi-colored rings in increasing size on a little pole; a blue dog with a book and a bone; a lovely peach teddy; a Raggedy Anne doll; a hand-knit bonnet and a woolen cap; two baby's first Christmas ornaments; a pink goose-down sleeping bag—a wise gift from my mother; a hand-knit jacket and matching slippers from her Irish godmother, Lucy; and last but not least a solid silver porridge bowl and a pair of gray suede shoes from her Californian godparents, Stephen and Danna.

Watching Deirdre sample all the treats before her was magical. She was cheerful and bright and intent on exploring her gifts. Our pretty one. She smiled and chatted to herself, occasionally looking our way with a nod as if to say, "Yes, yes, I'm very happy." And her warm little blueberry eyes looked steadily at us for a moment, seeing *us*: Mammy and Daddy. We knew we were doing it right.

CHAPTER NINE

How was it all going, then?

With Deirdre crawling with great and delighted urgency around the kitchen, picking up the tiniest speck of dirt, babbling innumerable sounds and gurgling and splashing madly as she lay out later in the little yellow tub before the fire, our images of Christmas were all happy ones. The days were full of quiet gladness. Everyone's happiness is different, and on a small farm in the west of Ireland ours was made of the tiniest things: carrying Deirdre out to see the hens, the endless naming of things for her and watching for the flicker of recognition across her face, the bumpy pram rides down the potholed road, the noiseless midwinter countryside, and the cattle nosing up to the walls to look out on the baby with the woolen hat on.

Deirdre's biological mother had signed the release papers, and now we were on the last nervy lap of the whole process. We were waiting to be called to Dublin for the final adoption order to be made legal. Up until the day we were called, Deirdre could be taken from us at a moment's notice, but through the celebration of Christmas we pushed that far from our minds.

"God is good," Mary said, "and please God ye'll have no troubles."

"Please God," I said, and meant it more than any prayer I ever uttered.

To take our minds from the worry, and to ease us past the middle of winter with laughter, warmth, and friendship, we had a flurry of visitors three days after Christmas. From London, my brother Paul arrived with his golf clubs and his rain gear; from New York, Chris's brother Sean; and from Chicago, her inimitable cousin, P. J. Brown.

For some time now, Chris and I had understood that for a little band of our closest friends and relatives, our continued living here had become a kind of light on the horizon. In some small way we were an emblem of hope or freedom or something, a counterimage of green fields, peace, and quiet, against those days when urban life rushed or pushed too hard and fast upon the spirit, and left a gnawing dissatisfaction inside. "Yes, we are still here, and never more happy," we would write, feeling as we did some responsibility for making other people's dreams true.

Kiltumper had come to seem a sort of relief post, quite literally a place apart, a place to come to in which to draw breath and look outwards across the fields, to find the direction of your life. Here, in the green and gray rain light, the world took on a different aspect. As elsewhere in the west of Ireland, time here seemed to slow to a standstill. Walking the winter roads in the drizzle, bringing in turf for the fire, or helping to close a gap the cows had broken through, P. J.,

Paul, and Sean easily slipped into the Kiltumper frame of mind. They were each at a turning point in their own life; Paul preparing to move from the world of London business to the challenges of America, Sean heading for Toronto in late January, and P. J. returning to Chicago to take up a difficult role in a hard-hitting Northern Irish play called *Ourselves Alone.* It seemed Kiltumper Cottage was the quiet eye in the whirlwind. And in those first days of the new year in our little home in the lulled west Clare countryside, there was the sense of being present at the birth of dreams.

Mugs of tea and wedges of Chris's Grandma Kitty's Fruitcake were the order of the day, and word games, chat, and music were our nighttimes. We had finally tracked down a futon in Dublin, and the new bedroom upstairs was at last in use. Ours was a full house now, and with the baby at its center the new year seemed to glisten with hope.

In a burst of serious holiday making a round of golf at Lahinch was planned. Of the four of us, only Paul could truly call himself a golfer. We decided to rise at first light and get on the first tee by nine o'clock, so as "to avoid the crowds." Chris happily volunteered to stay at home with Deirdre.

Daybreak in midwinter Ireland is not generally a spectacular affair. So often the light seeps out of the edge of the eastern sky and palely washes the morning with a watery gray at half past eight. As the Peugeot raced over deserted roads up to the fairways, the greens, and the very rough rough of Lahinch, it was that sort of day.

Lahinch golf course is rightly famous for several reasons: it's one of those wild blustery places that offer the golfer "a challenge" as he tees off into often gale-force Atlantic winds toward greens he cannot see. In the clubhouse, of course, he's told the white markers stuck into the sides and tops of grassy hills show the correct line of approach, and it is toward these rounded stones that he hacks, chips, and wallops his ball with all his force, watching what felt like a screamer sail off wide like a balloon in the whirl of an Atlantic breeze. Besides all this, there are such remarkable pleasures as the crisscrossing fairways of the Klondyke—upon which nobody has yet been killed; par fives that seem unreachable in eight or nine strokes; and the Dell, a simple little par-three hole in which the green lies hidden behind two high hills, deep in a kind of grass crater, and the ball rolling down to it inevitably rolls off it, too.

This was the course we had come to. In the parking lot there was no sign of anyone. The day was just beginning and off the sea a stiff breeze flapped at our pants. I remembered another curiosity about Lahinch as we carried our clubs up to the clubhouse: the goats. A little herd of white goats had wandered over the course for years now. There was a sign inside the clubhouse door about them and a piece of local lore that promised rain if the goats were down around the clubhouse. That morning, there, of course, they were. I said nothing, walked out to the tee, and walked back when I felt the wind. It was gusting right across the fairway, and while Sean and P.J. did their American-style warm-ups and Paul pulled on his rain pants and jacket, his glove and his cap, I watched the goats watching us.

"Right, I'll start," I said, and taking a long iron club, hit one of the best shots I have ever hit in my life.

"Look at that," teased Sean, "pretends he spends all his time farming and writing. Probably shooting golf balls up at the cows all winter!"

Ten minutes later, we were out on the course, and my sudden golf form had as suddenly collapsed. We were whacking balls along by the sea now, almost aiming them into the ocean and letting the breeze fly them in lovely soft arcs onto the grass. Or so I, at least, pretended, shaking my head disbelievingly at the skies as the wind sometimes dropped and my shot hooked sharply into the sea. By now we were a little farther out on the course and still there was nobody before or behind us; great hillocky slopes of grass rose and fell away endlessly before us. We were miles out there in the lovely lonely landscape with the seabirds screaming in the January morning overhead and the air gusting so fresh and clean that it blew the old year out of you.

Of course, at first, we hardly noticed it was raining. We hardly glanced at the black-black sky that overhung us and the village of Liscannor veiled in a downpour. We cracked the balls ahead of us and only gradually noticed our faces streaming with water. Wasn't that the sea spray? Besides, we were there to play golf, and, as any golfer in Ireland knows, you can't be put off by a little rain. These hills of rough, this roaring Atlantic breeze, this capricious pocked little ball of elastic that flew or piddled over the grass toward a bent-over iron pin in the distance, this slicing and hooking, hacking, whacking, bunkering, bogeying, double-bogeying and not-birdying, these four-man-hunts with wet shoes and socks in a thickly tufted undergrowth where the lost ball was imagined to have dropped and where only hares or birds might find it, wasn't this all part of the sport of it? Of course we carried on. On the ninth hole, we walked over to where the search had begun for P.J.'s ball and the four of us burst out laughing. The skies were lashing down on us. Sean pulled at the leg of his jeans; they were like wet weights on him now, and a small bluish trickle ran from them. On the tenth tee, unable to see anything through my glasses, I placed my ball to begin the back nine holes with a burst of energy. By now I had given up the delaying vanity of practice swings. I tried to remember all the essentials my father had taught me: head down, hand-grip, vee to the right shoulder, feet nicely spaced, easy backswing, don't hurry it, don't break the wrists, top of the arc, and then down easy, move the hips, keep the head down and follow through. Thwack! I hit a beauty. The ball shot like an arrow through the rain.

And so did my club!

Half an hour later, laughing with rain-washed faces and wetter than wet, the four of us walked back along the completely deserted course to where the goats were sheltering by the clubhouse.

"Not a bad game of golf," said Paul, with a smile, as we spread newspapers and coats across the car seats and lowered ourselves in out of the rain. The Peugeot sped back toward a different life in Kiltumper, where Chris had prepared a marvelous dinner. After bowls of thick soup, at last came Socky the turkey, and steaming basins of peas, potatoes, onions, carrots, followed by Chris's own plum pudding and fresh cream, a pot of tea, and a hearty slice of Grandma Kitty's Fruitcake.

The boys love Deirdre. I mean really, when you think of it, here are three young lads in their mid-twenties, without wives or children, crammed into this two-bedroom house in the middle of nowhere with an eight-month-old girl. Paul sleeps in the kitchen, so he's all right, but Sean and P. J. are living dangerously, sleeping right next to Deirdre's room, which is only partitioned off with plywood from theirs. When I think of it, it's a real character test for all of us. And so far, we're all first class. But Deirdre wins the prize. The boys can't believe how pleasant she is—all the time. Eight months *is* a wonderful time in a baby's life and even Niall and I are wondering, is it *all* going to be this easy?

We had a dilemma on the farm. Our goat, who had been with us for a little over a year now, had suddenly come "in season." "Noising" all the day, she skipped from the field to the road and trotted back and forth in a gathering frustration until eventually the poor cows crashed out over the wall to join her. Then, in a pack, they galloped off after the goat into someone else's farm. Twice in three days I had had to go searching for them.

Perhaps the obvious solution to the problem was to bring "a gentleman" visiting, and have the goat go in kid, as it were. But, as much as we liked having the goat on the farm, we didn't quite want to start rearing a flock of kids, and so put aside for now at least the idea of the gentleman caller. So, as always, we took our problem on the *cuaird* with us to our neighbors:

"You could take her off somewhere, up to north Clare maybe, where they have goats, and let her off."

Absurdly for a moment I glimpsed an image of our plain nanny finding a home with the aristocratic golfing goats of Lahinch.

"You could chain her up somewhere," said somebody else, "and she wouldn't be bothering the cows then."

"You could have her killed, and ask Paddy Cotter to make a *bodhran* out of her for you."

A *bodhran* is a traditional Irish drum instrument, made of goatskin stretched over a circular rim of timber. Chris grimaced at the thought of it. And so, for a couple of days we did nothing. Then, after wasting an hour one morning trying to discover where the blessed goat had led the cows this time, I felt furious and resolved to do something. I'd take her away in the back of the car that evening. I didn't care what the blazes happened to her, I was going to be rid of her.

I came into the kitchen and sat for coffee. Lucy arrived.

"What's the matter?" she asked.

Chris told her about our goat problem.

"Well now, whatever you do," said Lucy, "don't go throwing away that goat. Don't throw away your luck. Do you hear me?" She paused, sipped her coffee, and with only the hint of a smile, added: "You never know what might happen if you gave away your luck."

Don't give away your luck. In many ways the very idea of a lucky goat, of the mixed superstition and sentimentality that softened my resolve to get rid of the nuisance that afternoon, seemed to me another measure of how different things were here in the country. Because here of course was an element I hadn't counted on, the west of Ireland element, the lucky factor. For when somebody tells you not to give away your luck, how can you do otherwise but heed them? No, we wouldn't get rid of her. But we would have to try to slow her down, so that she wouldn't break out over the walls so easily.

"No problem," said Sean confidently. "have you a rope, Niall?"

I nodded and went to fetch it. So, with a length of rope knotted as a Wild Western lasso, Sean and I walked down the Kiltumper road in our Wellies like a couple of crusty rustlers. But we were out to round up a goat. By the time we entered the field near Downeses', we had a whole posse with us, Peter, Francie, Karol, Noel, Evelyn, Colette, and little Una, all galloping excitedly across the Fort Field to see what was happening.

"Are you going to catch her, Sean?" asked Francie.

"Yup," said the cowpoke with the lasso, picking out the goat as we headed over toward the herd.

Fanning out in a wide semicircle, and all stealing up as quiet as Indians, we slowly closed in on her. She was penned into a corner of the field before she realized it. Softly, Sean opened the lasso wide and lifted it over his head. There was a moment in which we all held our breaths and then he pitched it. A little quick swish sounded and then the rope flopped emptily onto the grass. Cool as you like, even as the rope had flown through the air, the goat had simply hopped over the wall. Karol burst out laughing.

"*Janey*, did you see that? She jumped over."

There was no use trying again. But we did. And again, too, closing in on her and having her skip away from us. We even gave up on the rope and in desperation tried to rush the poor animal and grapple her to the ground by her foot-long horns. Luckily, she was too fleet and clever for us, and the best we did was provide a kind of comic Wild West show there by the Fairy Fort. At length, Michael came out from his dinner to see how we were managing.

"What are you going to do with her, Niall?"

"I want to bring her up to the cabin and tie something onto her so that she won't be breaking out so easily."

"Well, you'll hardly catch her by herself. Why don't you bring all the animals back to the big cow cabin, and then you can separate her."

It was, of course, the right thing to do. Sean gathered the rope, and with the help of all the little Downeses we

174

drove the cows and the goat with rustler whistles and yelps back along the western road.

In the dim light of the cabin, the goat stood like a shadow with her head in a corner. This time she wouldn't escape us. Very very quietly, Sean leaned in and then suddenly grabbed her by the hindleg. She kicked out and thrashed and tried to shake free, but the two of us were upon her now, and, as she settled in our grasp, together we quickly tied a heavy chunk of timber to her horns.

"That should slow her down," I said, when we stood back to see how she took it.

"Yup," said Sean, watching her.

"Fellas, isn't it going to be difficult for her to move at all with her head weighed down like that?" asked Chris, peering in over the half door. "You should have tied it to her leg."

"No, no, she'll be fine," I said, "we don't want her to move very much anyway."

When I opened the cabin door, the cows trotted out onto the road and back down to their grazing in the Fort Field. The goat didn't budge. I yelled and raised the stick over her, trying to frighten her into motion, but it wouldn't work. She was stubborn as a mule and just stood there.

"Come on," said Sean, "we'll have to carry her down to the field."

And so, one of us holding the great heavy lump of timber that was roped around her horns, and the other bear-hugging the poor beast up off the road, we made our way slowly along after the cows. If anyone had seen us just then, I'm not sure I would have been quite able to explain just what we were doing.

"We're carrying your luck down the road," said Sean, trying to make the whole ridiculous business sound quite reasonable.

Yes, I was thinking. We're not throwing our luck away,

175

we're guarding it, we're saving every bit of it for the last agonizing part of our wait finally to be called to Dublin to finally adopt Deirdre. And in that light, for that reason, carrying a goat down the road with a piece of wood tied to its horns didn't seem so mad after all. We carried her into the middle of the field and set her down. Still she didn't move. A sudden fear that the weight might prove too great for her came over me. She wouldn't be able to drag it along, she wouldn't eat enough, she wouldn't get water. I'd come to check her in the morning and she'd be dead with a great hunk of ash tied to her head. What luck would we have then?

For five or ten minutes we stood there watching her. She didn't move a muscle. The cows came over to look at her curiously, and she still did nothing. What should we do? It seemed we had solved one problem only to make another. After a while, we gave up and went back to the house to think about it.

"I think you should cut it off her," said Chris. "What if she really can't move?"

"I'm sure she'll be able to move," I said. "I'll tell you what, if she hasn't moved by morning, I'll free her again, all right?"

"All right, but if she dies . . ."

If she dies. First thing the following morning, I woke and dressed in a hurry and walked down the road to the Fort Field full of nervousness about a goat. *Who could understand this?* In a way it was bound up with the precariousness of our life here, the very fine edge upon which our dream rested and the terrible uneasiness that is part of every adoptive parent's life until the final papers have been signed. This goat embodied all of that at the moment. I climbed the wall into the field by Martin Hehir's and hurried over the frosted ground. There was a blue spume of turf smoke from Downeses' chimney.

From the distance I could see she wasn't where we had left her. There was a muddy mark of stamping and dragging and a little trail through the frost. I was heartened, she was all right. But then I found the timber. She had chewed herself free of it and it lay now with a sad end of rope along by the side of the ditch.

Moments later, I came upon her grazing peacefully with the cows. About her horns was still a circle of the blue rope, fringed like a headdress or a punk hairdo. It was fantastic looking. In the weeks ahead she would wear it still, never breaking out of the fields again, staying quietly with the cows into the days of spring, and bearing the blue emblem of that piece of rope as a reminder always that she was the good luck that we hadn't been able to give away or tie down, but of her own will had come and simply stayed, and stayed.

Eileen and Phil Brown arrived today with gifts galore for us and for Deirdre. My cousin Kathy, from Florida, sent Deirdre a little plastic raincoat after reading about all the rain we had during our first two summers here. Eileen and Phil brought half a dozen *New York Times Magazines*, low-cholesterol homemade peanut butter, a chili mix, and pesto mustard (oh boy!) as well as some lovely things for Deirdre May. Eileen is my godmother and she and Phil, whom I still call Uncle Huck from childhood days, have been very supportive of our "adventure" from the start.

Huck wants to open a gallery on Martha's Vineyard and has asked me to contribute! I better start painting faster. I really have very little to show. They treated us, Sean and P. J., too, to a lovely dinner at the Old Ground, and before they left they bought one of my paintings for their collection. Now there's a gap on the wall, but money in the pocket, and today I'd rather have the money. But tomorrow, I'll start another painting even if it is January and dark and cold.

It was one of those squally wet January afternoons that wrap the Irish countryside in a ball of weather. Backsides to the breeze, the cows stood sheltering along the western wall, their hides glistening and running with rain. Like everyone else, they were a little mesmerized by the falling skies, the blown veils of gray that came and went in dull succession across the dead day. It was an afternoon after Christmas when farmers dropped into deep sleeps by turf fires, an afternoon when the children played with the colored bits and pieces of their toys, and ignored the downpour battering upon the windowpane outside. For Chris, Sean, P. J., and I, it was an afternoon to go and find some music. To hear pipes, tin whistles, and fiddles, jigging the air in a brown pub by the sea's side.

In the old blue Peugeot, thinking music and talking weather, we took our favorite road from Kiltumper — westwards to the ocean, then north by the rocks at Quilty. Driving by the edge of the Atlantic, the roads were so empty and sea-swept they seemed to run precariously along some middle world, a salty misted winter's place between land and sea. This was the west of Ireland, and here upon the western edge of Clare, as much as in the magical counties of Kerry and Connemara, Sligo, and Donegal, the shape and feel of the landscape evoked that special feeling that was all wildness and wind, a kind of tossed and solitary beauty that staggered and silenced the heart even as you drove through it. We sang snippets of a few ballads and hushed only as the road ran around by the beach at Spanish Point and there before us were the curling, crashing white waves of January. It was here the galleons and men-of-war of the Spanish Armada had foundered on the rocks centuries before.

From Spanish Point along the coast road to Lahinch, Sean sang over the rain and the wind. In half an hour's driving we had not passed a single car. At Lahinch, the beach is spectacular, stretching away past the famous championship golf course and curving with the green arc of Liscannor Bay. The old West Clare Railway used to bring thousands here on day trips from Ennis or other inland towns in those beginning days of the century when every man wore a hat or a cap and the women lifted skirts to paddle the shallow waves. The famous Lawrence photographs of the early 1900s show the scene: the muslin or cotton dresses, the wide-brimmed sun hats with a hand raised demurely against the breeze, and the splendid promenade that still lines the strand today. Of the railway however, only a few weed-strewn dilapidated trestles are left.

"What happened to it?" P. J. asked, as we took the road around Liscannor and headed for Moher.

"They took up the tracks in the fifties," I told him. "Apparently it wasn't a very effective train, and with trucks and lorries and the improved road system the need for it disappeared."

"And it wasn't very punctual!" Chris added.

"No, it wasn't. There was a famous poet, painter and composer, Percy French—"

"—And he wrote a famous song about it," Chris cut in again, " and it was called . . ." She looked at me, smiling broadly.

"*Are Ye Right There, Michael, Are Ye Right?*"

And so, launching into Percy French's comic tribute to the romantic steam engines of the West Clare Railway, we drove to the Cliffs of Moher under lightening, lifting skies.

You may talk of Columbus's sailing
Across the Atlantical sea
But he never tried to go railing
from Ennis as far as Kilkee.
You run for the train in the mornin'
The excursion train starting at eight
You're there when the clock gives the warnin'
And there for an hour you'll wait.

And as you're waiting in the train
You'll hear the guard sing this refrain:
"Are you right there, Michael, are you right?
Do you think that we'll be there for the night?
Ye've been so long in startin'
That ye couldn't say for certain
Still ye might now Michael, so ye might!"

They find out where the engine's been hiding
And it drags you to sweet Corofin
Says the guard, "Back her down on the siding
There's the goods from Kilrush comin' in."
Perhaps it comes in in two hours
Perhaps it breaks down on the way;
"If it does," says the guard, "be the powers
We're here for the rest of the day!"

And while you sit and curse your luck
The train backs down into a truck!

"Are ye right there, Michael, are ye right?
Have ye got the parcel there for Mrs. White?
Ye haven't! Oh Begorra!
Say it's coming down tomorra
And it might now, Michael, so it might!"

And so, on the song goes with the train, to Lahinch and Kilkee until the fall of evening and the journey home:

Kilkee! Oh you never get near it!
You're in luck if the train brings you back,
for the permanent way is so queer, it
Spends most of its time off the track,
Uphill the old engine is climbin'
While the passengers push with a will
You're in luck when you reach Ennistymon
For all the way home is downhill.

And as you're wobblin' through the dark
You hear the guard make this remark:
"Are ye right there, Michael, are ye right?
Do you think that we'll be home before it's light?"
"'Tis all dependin' on whether
the ould engine holds together—"
"And it might now, Michael, so it might!"

Chris and I have been to the Cliffs of Moher. We have taken many visitors there, and have never once come away uninspired. That afternoon, it was deserted. Wrapped in coats and hats we stepped out into the wind and walked down to land's end. Shrieking seabirds and the rushing sounds of the wash of the ocean were all around us. At the place where the flagstones were jammed upright as a long wall barrier before the drop to the sea, we shouted to be heard, and eventually stood silently listening. If you watched the ocean's churning six hundred feet below it seemed to foam and batter on the cliffs without a sound. Watching it, you could hear nothing when the waves crashed. Then, as if the volume was suddenly turned up, the terrific delayed noise rose and consumed the air. It was out of synchrony, and standing there on the cliff edge, so were we. There are spells and mystery in the wind at Moher, and just a touch of madness, a sense of how small you are and how immense and murderous are the winter waters of the Atlantic Ocean. We hurried mutely back to the car and drove on.

From Moher, we took the road that rises and curves northwards along the coast of Clare. Now, the sweep of Galway Bay was suddenly spread in front of us and the rock shapes of Aran lay humped in the rain light. What was it like out there on the islands on late wintery afternoons like this when the light fell so rapidly and the air was so full of sea, mist, and rain that the mainland must look shrouded in gray shadows?

In the little village of Doolin across from the Aran Islands, we stopped the old Peugeot and parked. Beyond the closed doors of O'Connor's there was music. And plenty of it. Late afternoon in the middle of winter in the holiday season, and there was a *seisiun* on inside the dark Guinness-colored pub.

As we came in, there were only a handful of people in the pub. One of the two bars was still closed, but along the narrow counter inside the door a little audience had gathered behind their pints. Down by a large, ornate wooden seat, known as the Piper's Chair, a band of musicians were arranged around a table and playing away on fiddles, tin whistles, guitars, accordions, and a *bodhran* drum. The whole place was full of their tune, as we sat down. We felt we had come into a jubilant haven, where, as they say in Clare, the "crack," or fun, was mighty.

A couple of thigh-slapping, foot-tapping jigs and a couple of reels, and then a slow air was played solo on the tin whistle. You could touch the quiet. You could hear the sea wind at the door and nothing else but the man at the whistle, fingering out a sadness that was so doleful it seemed sweet. Looking around at the faces of everyone there, I felt keenly the importance of the place in these people's lives. Here were a number of musicians, all quite poor, spending their days in Doolin and playing hours upon hours of Irish music for one reason alone; they were mad for it. There was little or no hope of wealth for any of them from the playing of these sounds, from all the learning and fingering and perfecting of skills. There was even little recognition for it, a few smiling faces, a few ripples of applause in a small pub in the west of Ireland. And yet, watching them, and listening there in O' Connor's that afternoon as the windows darkened and the music played on, I knew that for them this was all that mattered. This was the stuff for it, this was the business to get the worries out of your head and put the jizz in your feet. These were the tunes to be learned and played and passed on. They were and always will be the expression of this place, this green island in the eye of the Atlantic. And playing this music was the way of the West.

In the middle of the evening, a round-faced man with a gleeful smile sat down next to us, and I recognized Micko Russell, one of the legendary tin whistle players from Clare.

"How are you, Micko?" I said to him.

"Oh grand sure, grand," he said, looking around at the four of us. "Lovely bit of music they're playing."

"Yes," said Chris.

"'Tis, 'tis," he said, sitting back and listening.

I noticed the red mouthpieces of three tin whistles sticking out from his jacket pocket, but said nothing though I hoped that later he might play. At a lull in the music, the players put down their instruments a moment and pints aplenty came to their table from the bar. Micko, with his hands clasped on his knees, took their greetings as they passed us, and then, quietly, almost furtively drew out one of the tin whistles. With a little toot to start, he moistened his lips and held the whistle out from him again, as if somehow it, and not he, hadn't warmed up yet, and the music hadn't reached this narrow piece of tin tubing with the six holes. Then, with a blink and almost imperceptible little jig of the shoulder, he slipped it to his mouth and the melody danced. He was playing quietly, just for those around our table. But in listening to him, and imagining the near infinite number of tunes this big man had played in his lifetime, you sensed at once it didn't matter to him whom he was playing to or for; he was playing for the sheer joy of it. Reels and airs flew like magic from the tiny tin instrument in his fingers.

When he finished we thanked him.

"That's called 'Scattery Island,'" he said. "Do ye know where that is?"

"We do," I said. "Down by Kilrush."

"Down by Kilrush is right," he said. "Well now, the story of that is that down in Scattery Island there was a tower, do ye see, called Saint Senan's Tower. He was a great saint down there. Well, there was this woman down in Kilrush and every Easter Sunday she used to have Willie Clancy—ye've heard of Willie Clancy?—well, Willie Clancy and a few other musicians come down to Saint Senan's Tower to play that tune. It was Easter Sunday and the Resurrection of the Lord." He paused and looked up around him a moment. "And when they played that tune all the fishes would swim up around the tower there and dance a kind of Caledonian set on the water!! They played it at Easter after that and the little fishes would all dance."

He put the whistle to his lips again and started to play. A number of people were now standing around the table, and the pub had hushed. Halfway through a lilting tune, Micko stopped abruptly and turned to me.

"You're an educated man," he said. "Did you ever hear tell of Bunting, the musical collector?"

"No, I haven't," I replied.

Another man, with gray hair tufting from beneath his cap, was standing, listening, behind us and he said:

"That's right, Bunting, the musical collector."

"He went around Ireland in the seventeenth century collecting tunes and that," said Micko Russell. "That's a tune called 'The Catholic Boy.'"

"'The Catholic Boy' is right," said the man behind us.

"Well, some of those tunes, Micko, must be as old as the hills," I ventured.

"They are and more," said Micko. "Some of them, sure, are two and four hundred years old—that was the seventeenth century sure, and what are we in now . . ."

"The nineteenth century," the man behind us answered in all seriousness.

Nobody said a word to contradict him. There, in that nineteenth-century nighttime in Doolin, the music started up again. The rain outside was pouring into the pounding dark sea, but in the warm smoky air of the pub nothing mattered but the reels and the jigs, the hornpipes and the slow airs, and the dancing tunes kept alive by the efforts of a Mr. Bunting, the musical collector.

CHAPTER TEN

An American winter evening—Super Bowl Sunday, the Denver Broncos versus the Washington Redskins. Down the road, Peter and Francie had laughed aloud when they heard the names. "Who could we be, Niall?" asked Peter. "The Kiltumper Krushers?"

During the course of the winter, each week the Irish national television station, Radio Telefis Eirinn, had broadcast a one-hour program of American football. One game was compressed into sixty minutes of edited highlights. In Ireland, we only heard rumors of the marathonlike three-hour football-viewing sessions with commentary, analysis, time-outs, and commercial breaks. On our "Touchdown" program there were no delays between plays, no ads, no boring plays or dull spells, but only a cavalcade of spectacular runs and passes, of superhuman figures hurdling into the end zones or giantly shouldering their way to first downs. As well as all this, we were treated to a weekly five-minute rundown of results and shown two or three of the most spectacular plays in each game. It was all a feast of successes, of celebratory American moments with the quarterback acting like some old western gunslinger and the fans chanting like so many Indians. To the Irish nation in wintertime, the weekly image of this American game played in the spotlight on a perfectly lined greener-than-green surface without bumps or puddles, was one of fast, fearless action, daring and extraordinary athletic feats.

Then came Super Bowl Sunday, the Denver Broncos versus the Washington Redskins. By now, in Ireland, despite an initial scoffing at those mad Yanks in their tight pants and big shoulderpads (couldn't they wear ordinary knicks and jerseys like proper men?), there was a small but solid audience of American football supporters. The country even boasted a handful of amateur teams, among them the Dublin Celts, who had managed to meet the considerable cost of securing playing gear and were now committed to starting an Irish mini league. So, if not with all the hype and anticipation that greeted it in America, Super Bowl XXII was eagerly awaited. What's more, it was being televised *live*. From the various highlights seen through the autumn, teams had attracted their own Irish supporters, not infrequently because the quarterback might be called O'Brien or McMahon, or because a brother or sister had emigrated to New York or Chicago and sent home a Giants, Jets, or Bears sweatshirt.

By ten o'clock in the evening, Irish time, the broadcast was ready to begin. A Super Bowl party had commenced in the television studio in Dublin and a number of our famous international rugby players had been called in as "experts." With rain lashing against the windows outside and Deirdre asleep in the back bedroom, Chris made a great big bowl of popcorn on the Stanley range, and acted as our resident expert.

Suddenly, we were handed over from dark rainy Dublin to Pasadena, California. The picture showed a festive world of bright colors, banners, flags, mascots, and cheerleaders. From Kiltumper we were transported to the scene of the premier American football game. Between the glow of the turf fire in Clare and the dazzling sunshine of California lay all the difference in the world. In Ireland that week all the talk had been of government cutbacks in health and education, of austerity drives, of tightening our belts, lowering inflation and saving the economy. We were worrying about unusually high rainfall figures for January. There on the screen, warming up in the sunshine, glittered the helmeted champions of America.

The game began with the fastest touchdown in Super Bowl history. This much I think I will always remember. From the American commentators facts flooded over us, such-and-such a player had such-and-such an average on first downs, so-and-so had made so many yards this season. The viewers were kept vastly informed, and into the many natural breaks and stoppages in the game came what seemed an important secondary part of the whole business: the figures. In Ireland, sports commentators rarely even mention a player's age. His weight or height, the combined poundage of the defensive players for Kerry, say, or the average distance of the *sliothar* when cracked by the finest Kilkenny hurler, are all unknown facts. Parts of the televised games actually unfold in silence.

So then, it can only barely be imagined what effect the volumes of statistics, facts, the weights and yards, the charts and diagrams, and the little X's and O's and arrows that suddenly appeared over the slow motion replays, had on the Irish nation as it sat up late on a rainy Sunday night to watch the Super Bowl. At the end of the first quarter, we were "handed back" to Dublin. One of our rugby experts said how well the game was going, how exciting it was. And then, the host of the program turned face on to the camera to speak to all those across the country watching and wondering at the incredible spectacle. There had been a number of phone calls, he said. One question kept coming up (When he stated it, it seemed to me to elucidate the whole difference between the spirits of Ireland and America): tell me why, said the callers, do they keep on running with the ball bang into the other fellas? Why the blazes don't they just pass sideways? Then they wouldn't need to be spending money on all those helmets, now would they?

One lone, fat anemone bud is sheltering among a cushion of creeping arabis. One of these days it's bound to open—if the rains and winds ever ease up. It's been a mild winter so far, but oh, so wet.

Today, after a long month of heavy rain which has left fields glistening with tiny puddles, the afternoon cleared to a solid blue sky. As I write in my journal my arms and back are sore and tired from a burst of gardening—my first of the new year. I pruned the roses and cut back the deadened stems of the hardy perennials. The primulas are blooming and the strong, straight leaves of the crocus, daffodils, iris, and snowdrops are several inches above the soil. The Japanese onions (winter onions) have survived so far, and although they look a bit frail it is encouraging to see their rows of greenery in a mostly naked garden. It was invigorating to be outside. After I returned to the cottage I thought of the groundhog in New York who was deciding whether or not to stay inside. But today, I grabbed the blue day and let the sun shine down on me.

Shortly after midday, I walked outside in the still February air to find Mary scurrying toward me. "Niall, there's a big wind coming," she said in a kind of urgent whisper, and crossed to the cow cabin. "You want to make sure all the doors are secured tightly for fear the roof'd blow off 'em." As we stood talking, there was hardly a breath of wind. The leafless trees spread motionlessly beneath a clear blue sky and I had even been thinking it would soon be time for spring planting. It hardly seemed possible that such a "big wind" was coming. And yet, Mary knew best, and in a sudden hurry I helped her check all the cabin doors and windows, knotting the old half-door shut with baler's twine and tying it to a wedge of timber jammed in a crevice between the stones. This was like getting ready for a hurricane, I thought. As Mary hopped on her bike and pedaled away down the road, I went inside to tell Chris.

Half an hour later I drove down to Kilmihil for groceries and a newspaper. In the post office, the postmistress, Mrs.

Fitzgerald, was earnestly searching through the *Irish Press* for something of grave importance.

"Did you hear any weather forecast, Mr. Williams?" she asked me, looking up and peering over her glasses.

"No," I said, "only that somebody said there's a storm supposed to be coming."

"There is," she said, and finding her spot, read from the paper, "'Increasing winds off the west coast, gale force eight expected.'"

Ten minutes later, I was in Frank Saunders' shop at the top of the street.

"Did you hear anything about a storm?" I asked him.

"Yes," he said, "there's some talk of a storm all right. Mind you the barometer read 'Fair' this morning."

"But it's so still out," I said. There wasn't a cloud in the sky. It was in fact the best day's weather in almost a month. Just in case, I bought four white candles from where they had been moved up to the front of the counter, and a spare box of matches. Driving home from the village, I thought I noticed small signs of preparation everywhere, cattle being herded down off high places, half sheets of black plastic being tightened over the tops of hay ricks, clamps of turf being covered, a car going home with two cylinders of heating gas sticking out of the trunk. Were these things coincidental? Or was there really a sense of making ready before "the big wind"? I couldn't say. In two winters in Kiltumper we thought we had experienced every variety of blown rain, sleet, and hail, but we had never known anything like this tightening and tying down, this hill and sky watching, this country-wise respect for what the weather might do.

At ten o'clock that evening I stepped outside the back door to take a look. The sky was not full of stars, but there were sprinkles of them, like so many fists of glitter thrown upon the deepest blue. Only the barest whisper of a breeze was blowing, the gentlest whooing of a wind, breathing a lullaby through the winter nighttime across the darkened fields and valleys. There was nothing to indicate a storm. I went inside and told Chris there was nothing to worry about.

At three o'clock in the morning, a terrific roaring woke me from sleep. At first I thought it had been a man's cry, one of those long agonizing sounds out of nightmare of a body falling through bottomless dark. But no, there it was again. Chris stirred beside me, then shot upright.

"Niall, what is that?"

"It's wind," I said, moving to the dark window and listening to an incredible howling in the ash and sycamore trees behind the house.

"It sounds terrible," said Chris. "Niall, it'll blow the roof off!"

"No, it won't," I said, having no real idea whether it would or wouldn't. "The roof on this house is fine, we'll be all right." And yet, lying back into bed, eyes wide open and ears humming with the blasting of unruly air, we both half-expected the whole upstairs room to go sailing off into the swirling nightwind, if one of the great trees outside didn't crash through the roof first. After ten minutes lying there, listening to a very loud and continuous screeching, Chris sat up.

"We can't sleep up here," she said. "For one thing, it's too noisy, and for another, I'm scared. Plain and simple. Let's go down to the kitchen."

We peered in at Deirdre, still sleeping soundly with one arm tight around the red Christmas teddy, then made beds for ourselves in the kitchen before the last glowing of the fire. The windows were whistling. The curtain on the front door was billowing, and as I lay down on the floor I felt a brisk draft of cold air whisking across the linoleum. There were drafts and counterdrafts, gusts and blasts all over the house, and to lie there with the storm whirling outside was to feel every one of the two-hundred-year-old stones of the place actually breathing like a runner against the wind.

By morning the electricity was out. On weak batteries the radio at full volume barely competed with the roar of the wind. It announced a staticky warning: a major storm was sweeping the country, gale force ten winds had steadily increased over the course of the night and were now expected to reach storm force ten, hurricane force, by midday. Power lines were down, electricity was off up and down the country, high tides had washed parts of coastal roads into the sea, cars had blown over, trees were down everywhere. It was dangerous to go out; it was the worst storm in years.

In the dim light of the February morning, we lit a fire in the big hearth in the kitchen. Without electricity, we couldn't use the Stanley, for the water pump was out and we had previously heard stories of exploding boilers and other such horrors from the use of a range when the current was off. Our only fallback was the crook and crane over the old-fashioned fire on the floor. With the wind gusting terrifically, the smoke flew up the chimney and the turf blazed a little light. Chris put Deirdre's bottle of milk into the pitch-black kettle overhanging the flames and then went to get her from her bedroom.

Half an hour later I was ready to go outside. From the kitchen window we could see no apparent damage around the house. The roof was still on, only a few medium sized branches of ash had come down, and the car was still in one piece. But what of the animals? It was a February morning and the cows would be hungry for hay. I hadn't herded them down to the cabins, and at the sound of the wind at the back door, for a second I actually imagined airborne cows being blown over hedges. I turned the knob and the door was flung in on me. A step outside and my breath was gone. I literally couldn't breathe into the face of it and turned to walk backwards out into the yard. Above me, the roaring in the branches raged like an amplified sea of sound, like a world thrashing in anger, like nothing I had ever heard before. There was a kind of aching in the treetops, a tremorous resistance. Twigs would suddenly fly off into the air and old forked branches were bent backwards, like overdrawn catapults, against the sky. Around the corner of the back of the house the wind blew like mad. I reached the cabins and found the doors blown in on two of them. But snuggled in on top of themselves in a corner, the hens were all right.

Then to the haybarn. Birds were sheltering in the eaves of the corrugated iron roof. As I came in to take a bale, they scattered out into the air and then screamed and cawed in a kind of baffled, backward-blown flight as the wind took them. With the hay on my back, stepping out into the Kiltumper road, I couldn't help but feel giddy with the enormity of the storm. My windy-steps staggered drunkenly. I felt light, marvelously diminished to nothing more than leaf weight by the huge power of this gale. I let out a shout, a long aaaaahhhhh at the top of my lungs, that wasn't heard ten steps away. Man was nothing in weather like this. The world was all blown asunder and swept clean. I walked by the spruce trees across from the house knowing that at any second I might hear the crack of timber overhead. Down the road, telephone poles were at ten o'clock angles to the ground, and great loops of wires were swinging loose. And from gaps in the "fencing" of our fields I saw that furze bushes and blackthorn trees had been blown away.

I found the goat and the cows standing huddled all together in a corner, heads down against the bushes. They didn't even lift their eyes for the hay. I pulled off the two strands of baler twine and wisps and more wisps of hay whirled past them into the air.

The wind seemed to be strengthening. Suddenly, tracer bullets of large hailstones popped and snapped about my ears, whitening the road in a second and then fading away even as my footprints stamped a trail across them back to the house. Ahead of us was the darkest February day, a cold, cut-off, lone morning, afternoon, and evening, with buckets of water drawn from the well, no light or stove, and man, woman, and child sitting in the kitchen before the open fire, with candles, turf smoke, and the slow gradual noise of the watched kettle's boiling hiss.

The storm they call Storm K has eased away into the North Sea. We are still without electricity and running water after two days. A fire burns hot and strong on the floor of the open hearth and boils the water for Deirdre's meals. The kitchen is dark and lit only by the shadowy flickering firelight.

The hurricane winds have done much damage throughout the country. Locally, electricity poles have fallen over. We are lucky. Everything is standing, roofs still attached, hay and dwindling turf in place. It is in the garden that damage has been done. Everything is wind burned. Even the hardy leaves of the santolini and lavender and curry plant are blackened and withered. Any growing green thing brave enough to make an early spring appearance has been burnt to blackness. The poor old holly tree looks like a giant spindly skeleton.

Nothing to be done. Outside another storm is brewing, but the hurricane winds have weakened. Niall, who sits in his chair by the fire writing a letter, looks up and out the window. "It's snowing slightly," he says.

It was forty-eight hours before the lights came on again. In the blasted, brown aftermath of the storm, spring seemed a far place. For days upon days, cold rains swept down over us and the puddled fields were mucked brown under the hoofs of cattle. Damage was being repaired everywhere. Haybarns had been unroofed, trees felled. We passed many farms with men in their haggards or yards slowly remending the world for spring.

Down at the school, three wintry days a week, I was still teaching English. So far, a school play had been produced, a few in-school radio programs of chat and music had been recorded, and now, with the youngest pupils, we were working on writing short stories. The day after the storm, the weather beating all morning against the windows, three or four late boys sitting at the back of the class with hair rain-plastered and clothes drenched to the skin, I thought of the windy adventure we had all just lived through and asked the class to write a story beginning "The most amazing thing happened yesterday . . ."

I was wondering what it must have been like to have

been born and lived here always, to have walked the empty road to school or cut across the fields in seed-flecked, wet-legged trousers. What storms and blizzards, what wet springs and lost summers had washed themselves into the souls of the young.

Later, I read the stories. None of them even referred to the storm. One began: "The most amazing thing happened yesterday. It was a bit windy out and I went visiting my Uncle John." All the rest were set in dazzling sunshine.

Meanwhile, for Chris and for me, these again were waiting days. Springtime bore the promise of Deirdre's adoption—or the loss of her. Soon, we would drive to Dublin, to go before the Adoption Board. There, if passed by the six or seven members of the Board, Deirdre's legal papers would be signed, and the whole long, anxious process would be over. But we knew from Helen that until the day we were called—indeed, until the very moment that the adoption order was made and the papers were signed—the baby could still legally be taken from us.

Feeling the insecurity of not being "natural" parents (How I hate that distinction. What were we, "unnatural" parents?) and having to go on a kind of final parental interview with the baby in our arms, we were both filled with an uneasy, fretful worry at the thought of going to Dublin. We were good parents after all. Deirdre was happy with us. But would the Board be able to tell that just by looking at her? What if she wouldn't sit still or became cranky? Then what use would it be for us to assure them that she was a perfect baby, laughed every day, ate well, and slept all night? Imagining ourselves in some way inferior to other parents, we hardly dared trust our own instincts. We didn't *want* Deirdre to cry when we handed

197

her over to a stranger to hold, but when she didn't, did it mean something? Was she indifferent to us? It seemed she was happy to be in anyone's arms. Always pleasant and giggly. Suddenly now, in the last waiting weeks of February, the entire process of adoption seemed concentrated. In the baby's every sound and gesture we looked for signs.

Each day she was secured into the Baby Bouncer that was suspended from the kitchen ceiling. There she dangled just to the ground, practicing a kind of walking ballet for an hour at a time and laughing in delight as she raised a leg and let herself swing or pirouette in air. Now when we held her her legs seemed strong, and yet she kept up on her toes like a dancer. She absolutely wouldn't put her feet flat on the ground. Was this because of the Baby Bouncer? "Who knows," said Chris, "maybe they've found out in America that these things are bad for babies. Maybe they're banned!"

In this anxious and vulnerable state then, even the simplest things could topple us into panic: the news that playpens were considered psychologically unhealthy in some circles, the idea that babies should decide their own sleeping times, that sucking a thumb at bedtime should be stopped at once, or that you should never, never, never let a child cry. We listened, and worried about everything. But in the main we kept to what Chris called the old-fashioned way. Deirdre sat each morning in her playpen for two hours, amusing herself with colored boxes or beakers or her dolls, she put her thumb in her mouth when she was tired and was put to bed at seven o'clock every evening, giggling, not crying, as she lay down in the back room, and sleeping without a sound until morning. This was our baby at home in west Clare.

But how would the Dublin Board know?

An offical brown envelope arrived by post today, its contents informing us that we were expected in Dublin at the offices of the Adoption Board on Merrion Square on March 3 at 12:00. We were to bring baby Deirdre May with us. This is it. One week left to go. My God, will we ever last it?

I wonder what Deirdre will think when she grows up and we recount to her all our anxiety. What will she think about this very account? Deep in my heart I hope she will look at us gently, and even laugh and say, "Oh, Mom, you're silly. Didn't you know that I was always meant for you? I love you very, very much. Kiss. Kiss. Kiss."

CHAPTER ELEVEN

Everything was focused on getting ready now. All of our friends and neighbors, who had shared the wait with us, now shared in our mixed fearfulness and joy. "You've been called to Dublin? Oh, thank God, isn't it marvelous? I'm sure it'll all go well for you. Please God, it will." And so, at last, like a long worrisome pregnancy, we were coming to the end. Through one fine summer and a long wet winter a fierce and tender love had entwined little Deirdre into our lives. And now, the energy of that love ran like a charge through the remaining days. For the journey up and the interview in Dublin, nothing would be overlooked; in waves of suddenly released happiness, I realized I was smiling, just smiling, walking across the drizzled fields to check on the cows. It felt like I was preparing for a wedding or a birth, and yet, amidst the coming and going, there was always a fear that something might still go wrong.

Everything, of course, was to be done properly, with due ceremony and importance. In the kitchen, Chris was setting out a selection of Deirdre's dresses.

"Niall," she said, as she held them up in the air on their miniature hangers, "have you thought about the car?"

"The car?"

"Yes, go out and take a look at it. It's filthy. We can't drive up to Merrion Square with it looking like that."

On the dunged, mucked, and potholed country roads of west Clare, the washing of cars had seemed quite futile to me, and the Peugeot had not seen soap in two years since the morning I drove to Dublin and woke to find my father hosing it down to see what color it was.

"We'll never get it clean," I said.

"We'll have to, Niall. Couldn't you ask Michael Fitz? For Deirdre?"

I couldn't imagine it being done, but the following morning, on my way to school, I drove the old mud-caked Peugeot down the village to Fitzpatrick's garage. Michael walked out to me in his green overalls and rubbed his hands on a rag.

"How much? Ten pounds worth, is it?" he said, reaching for the pump.

I didn't really need the petrol, but let him pump it anyway while I got ready to make my request.

"Not a bad day," he said, glancing up the village and watching the gauge clock up five pounds.

"No," I said, "not bad at all."

"She's going well for you?" he asked matter-of-factly.

"She is," I said, and paused briefly before adding: "Any chance, Michael, you could give her a wash and clean?"

The gauge clocked ten pounds and he replaced the petrol cap and walked the pump back to its place before saying anything. Returning to the side of the car, he stood with me and then moved the toe of his black boot against the thickly baked on mud on the underside of the front panel. It made no mark.

"Inside and out?" he said.

"Inside and out," I replied, seeing a flash in my mind's eye of all the miscellaneous things and creatures that had traveled the Kiltumper road inside that car, chickens dead and alive, bowls of their blood on the backseat for Mary to make puddings, bags of turf, wood shavings for the floors of the hen cabin, rocks from the Burren, plants from everywhere, chairs and stools for parties, a butter churn, a flail, a creel and innumerable other set props for the Kilmihil Drama Group, a frightened cat and box of cat litter, a piddling puppy, a clutch of cow needles, a squeezing iron for castrating bullocks, a heating iron for burning the horns out of their heads, countless dirty diapers, and buckets of well water that slopped a little onto the floor as we sometimes picked up Joeso on his way back from the well.

This time the pause seemed longer. Then:

"Four o'clock alright?" said Michael.

"Four o'clock would be fine," I said.

In a freshly shampooed and unbelievably gleaming navy blue Peugeot, we left Kilmihil that afternoon on one of the most important journeys of our lives. In a way it seemed matched with the first long and adventurous journey that had brought us out of the office blocks of New York to the wilds of Clare. We had come then seeking a new life here, and now, as the car flashed east across the country a better life was what we wished for still. Ennis, Limerick, Nenagh, Roscrea, Mountrath, Portlaoise, Monasterevin, and on to Dublin. It was the reverse of the way we had come three years before, with a carload of suitcases but without the slightest idea of what lay before us: the grief of childlessness, the two deluged summers of rain, the cold stone house, and the puddled jungle of a ruined garden. Now, Deirdre slept in the backseat, and I drove very, very carefully.

If she got her usual night's sleep, Deirdre should be fine at the interview. Tips on traveling with babies ran through my head. We were both so anxious that everything go right that it seemed whole catalogs of essential "baby stuff" ran through our minds: the warming of bottles (I'd left the electric bottle-warmer in Kiltumper); spare nipples (I had brought four, in case we lost three); creams and powders for nappy rash (Deirdre's rear end was presently pinkly perfect, but what if she flared up overnight? *What if they wanted to check?*); baby blankets (Would she need them in the centrally heated house? Blankets could suffocate a child! Or was that just pillows?); jars of Beef Hotpot and Lamb Casserole and Pure Fruit (Or were we not supposed to be feeding shop-bought food anymore? Had they found out it was terribly damaging or deficient or something, and only the poor idiots out in the West were still not in the know?); and, of course, dolls (Two, brightly dressed and smiling, with no eye buttons to pull out and swallow and choke on).

By the time we pulled into the driveway of my parents' house in Kilmacud and Deirdre woke up in the backseat with a start, I couldn't help feeling a little terrified at the myriad responsibilities of parenthood, and newly awed at the miraculous wisdom that mothers and fathers possessed.

Tonight as I sit down to recollect the day I can barely remember what kind of day it was except that I know the sun was shining through a partly cloudy sky and it wasn't cold and through the green iron gates of the park at Merrion Square daffodils were trumpeting. It took us barely ten minutes to get from the Williamses' to Merrion Square, but we had to circle the block several times in search of a parking place. We were like an aircraft with anxious passengers after a long, long flight circling in for a perfect landing. I remember changing Deirdre's nappy in the backseat . . . and thank heavens I did! Then, just outside the Adoption Board office there was a handy bin, waiting for dirty nappies from lucky little babies about to be adopted. Funny, the things you remember. Our appointment was for 12:00, and at five minutes to noon we knocked on the blue Georgian door at 65 Merrion Square with our treasure in my arms.

She was dressed in a purple velvet smock (a gift from my oldest friend, Eileen Lynch) that has little green appliqued apples along a border. She wore a little white cotton blouse and white tights that I had bought from the Children's Corner in Mount Kisco—the shop where my mother had bought my clothes when I was a child. She had a little white sweater from Phyllis, her baby-sitter, and little white leather shoes that kept falling off. She was happy and looked about at everything with wide blue eyes.

Standing before the door I couldn't help but think of Dorothy in the tale of the Wizard of Oz standing before the door of the Emerald City with the Tin Man and the Scare crow and the Lion, waiting to be granted her wish. Where were my ruby slippers? We rang the bell and waited. A graying gentleman in a blue suit welcomed us warmly. Then he asked simply, "You are . . .?"

"The Williamses," we answered timidly and eagerly.

"Ah," he said, and motioned us through the door. We were guided into a room and asked to wait. No one else was there. No, this wasn't the boardroom and we breathed again and sat to wait out the last moments of our adoption-pregnancy. The room was high-ceilinged with white molding and sky-blue walls. Long white windows overlooked Merrion Square garden. It was a crawling baby's paradise with a thick rich carpet of royal blue.

Deirdre was happy bouncing on my knee. But there wasn't much time to play because within moments we were ushered into a larger high-ceilinged room. The moment we had been waiting for since June 30, 1987 was here.

Color and detail escape my memory. All I can remember is what I felt like. New life was about to be granted to me. Inside the room there was an enormous wooden table that stretched from end to end, circled by chairs seating a whole lot of people. All I remember was that everybody was smiling. A handsome woman spoke to us cordially. Then we were asked to swear on the Bible, and the man who announced himself as the registrar addressed us officially and asked a rotation of questions. Were we who we said we were, did we live where we said we did, were we residents of Ireland, had we resided there for the past twelve months, were we over twenty-five, did we marry on July 18, 1981, had we been married before, and finally, what was our religion? A paper was placed before us and the two of us asked to sign it. Niall signed first and when I held the pen, with Deirdre encircled in my left arm, and tried to write I realized that I was trembling all over. I could barely steady my hand to sign my name. Then the Board members asked us about Deirdre. Was she happy? She was particulary happy that moment. Did she know what was happening? I looked down to her. She was busy with two large plastic beads, a green one and purple one, that interlocked. "See for yourselves," I said. For a moment we all looked at Deirdre May, our little treasure, our pot of gold, and beamed. The handsome lady said, "All dressed up for the special day. How many teeth?" "Four," Niall said proudly. A brief silence stilled the room and all the people in it while we shared in a tremendous feeling of love. Then, finally, the registrar said, "Well, Mr. and Mrs. Williams, the Board and I are pleased to make an adoption order on your behalf for Deirdre May. Congratulations."

Niall turned to me and kissed me. It is all over. Deirdre is ours!

We left that lovely Georgian building on Merrion Square and stepped out as a family into the bustle of Dublin. Everything felt new. Across the road, by the park railings, a light spring breeze rustled in the year's first leaves. There were cars and road workers and lorries and buses and all the dust and noise of a usual city day, and yet, in the memory we hold of it now, these things seemed to float by like a lovely, silent parade. Nothing in the whole world was as real then as our feeling of joy.

It was millennium time in Dublin; the city was celebrating the one-thousandth anniversary of its founding. Into the heart of its festive streets we drove our old Peugeot like a good news chariot. A hundred times I looked at Chris and she looked at me and we both looked at Deirdre. We took turns carrying the baby. Her eyes opened wide and her head spun around to see everything and everyone: newspaperboys crying *Herald* or *Press*, fruit stalls, flower sellers, cheap jewelry hawkers, clothes, book and gift shops, crowds of swirling people, and babies everywhere in big comfortable prams and strollers rolling down wide, flat pavements that had no bumps or potholes. What did she make of the capital city that day? She laughed madly at her first sight of a big orange double-decker bus.

Bus, Deirdre, see the bus. Deirdre see the bus.

We felt that Deirdre had in some almost imperceptible way changed toward us, that she seemed happier, livelier, more free and at ease herself. Could she actually have known what this trip to Dublin meant? Or was it that she sensed that the anxiety we had felt was over now? Her lovely blue eyes danced. We took her to a small restaurant on Nassau Street for lunch, and she laughed at spaghetti and charmed the waitresses and customers all around her. Later, we visited an old friend, Marianne, in her boutique on St. Anne's Street, and again Deirdre seemed the happiest child in the world. She laughed at colors, clothes, sounds, and people. She had fits of it, putting back her head in mimic of me and giving a kind of hammed-up giggle that began deep in her belly and shook every inch of her. By four o'clock, we were walking back to the Peugeot. Jackhammers were pounding at a street corner. Our baby only smiled, laid back her head, and fell sound asleep in her mother's arms.

CHAPTER TWELVE

We first arrived here in the springtime, so it seemed that now we measured time in springs, in the daffodils of so many Aprils, and the deepening green of the grass on the hill fields of Tumper. Each springtime had already been an anniversary of hope for us. In late March each year we remembered the overgrown garden we had first walked into, the riot of scutch grass across the path and the nettles that grew thigh-high down by the hedgerows. We saw ourselves once again looking through the kitchen window at the absolutely empty room, our one chair and borrowed table, and looking out at the great lump of cow dung that was then the rhubarb bed. Each springtime we looked back and remembered: the hope that had been ours setting potatoes in thickly manured furrows in front of the house for the first time, the yearly battles against blight. This ground belonged to us now—or we to it. There was a bond, a bridge of April memories, of each year's attempt to make a further impression upon the stuff of muddy earth.

I had long shied away from the word "gardening," even before we arrived in Clare, as carrying with it a whole slew of dismissive associations, of Saturday afternoons pottering around the garden *passing the time,* whiling away retirement by potting up the occasional geranium, spraying a few roses, and picking apples. It was a word associated in my mind with watering cans, lawn clippings, and hedge trimmings, with the notion that "gardening" was a fine and harmless hobby, but not as important as, say, golf, and lighter work at that.

Passing the time? Here in Kiltumper, with each new spring we reviewed exactly how we had passed our time since our arrival. I had sweated through three Aprils by Chris's side, hacked, mucked, dunged, forked, and shoveled for all I was worth, falling into a chair in the evening with new blisters and a hunger that would empty a sack of potatoes. I was not the same person who had stepped from the commuter train each morning and walked up Park Avenue to 56th Street in sports jacket, gray flannel pants, and blue or white button-down oxford shirt. Nor was Chris the woman who had walked beside me, high heels in a bag and a cup of light coffee-to-go in her hand. We had both undergone, if not a sea change, a kind of earth shift. We were marked now with the dirt that wouldn't quite wash out of our fingers, with little bloodied scars where the old-fashioned roses and the briers had flayed the skin from our forearms; and marked, too, by the long quiet hours in this very quiet place where, in the hope of reaching and moving someone who was somewhere out there over Hayes' Hill, we had tried to write and paint.

Now, through Deirdre, everything in our lives seemed

marvelously renewed. There was a radiance to the days that made our old stone house seem at times a castle of dreams. These feelings were, I suppose, the commonplace stuff of new parenthood. But the world outside lent itself to these feelings. Suddenly the sun shone over Kiltumper for days on end. Our cows-in-calf lay out on the lower field as the startling yellow blossoms of the furze bushes blazoned the hills once more. The flowers shot up in the Easter garden, and Chris daily carried Deirdre out to see them. Chris had already drawn up this year's garden plan. The day after she had showed it to me, I lifted my head from writing to hear her outside telling Deirdre where the new plants would go. Listening, the simplest sweetest happiness washed over me and I thought: in all the days ahead may we never lose the light of this April joy.

Today, April 1, 1988, Deirdre walked straight across the kitchen! She's officially walking now. And she was so delighted with herself, laughing all the way, her arms outstretched. She turned at the couch and headed back toward Niall, practically running, on her tiptoes half the time, but keeping her balance. And if that wasn't exciting enough, we were in the garden today in *T-shirts*! Deirdre, too. It was another blue blue day and I mean blue skies— sunny skies.

When the weather turns good like this I always experience a sense of panic. There are a million things to do on such a lovely day. Gardening. An outing at the beach. Painting or sketching. Not to mention household chores. In Ireland there's something about a blue sky and dirty laundry that go together like tea and scones, or bread and butter. I feel a bit guilty if I let a clear day pass without hanging up a clean wash on the line in the haybarn. But this afternoon saw us out in the garden. First things first, after all. Pamela Blake, our young friend and baby-sitter, was minding Deirdre inside. The baby is a terror outside; she picks all the flowers. Niall and I worked in different parts of the garden; he dug potato ridges and I weeded the flower borders. The sun was shining in a clear blue sky. Our arms were bare to the warm air. What more could we ask for? I had such a feeling of wholeness and happiness. I hope in the years to come I can look back on this day and remember how good it is.

For Chris, the fine weather brought a new urgency to paint. There had been so many days through the winter when the light was a murky grayness and the rain against the window made the outside world colorless. Between Deirdre and the dullness, work on blank canvases had all but stopped. On the easel in the parlor, a large Connemara landscape (a desolately lovely road winding through Maam Valley in the shadow of mountains) had stood untouched for months. Now, in the heady sunshine of April, the painting was set up outside on the garden path and finished in a week. Another, of the cleanly dug ridges and first flowers of the spring garden, was begun almost at once. This, I knew, was the way Chris worked in

April. She found her rhythm in the springtime air and accomplished more in four weeks than in all the winter months together. At a rush then, in a mood of excitement, she called Chris O'Neill at Lisdoonvarna.

We had heard about Chris O'Neill's Burren Painting Centre two years before. Situated in the north Clare spa town of Lisdoonvarna, it was a place where painters from all over the country gathered for long weekends, going out into the spectacular Burren landscape with a tutor, and painting all day. Up until now, Chris had never quite managed to find the time to get away from the farm, the garden, and her own painting. But now, in the almost unbelievable glimmering of this year's spring in Ireland, the light drew her to the Burren.

In the Burren, 350 square miles of limestone plateaus and mountains are home to wild flowers found nowhere else in the country. It is one of Ireland's magical places. Like Glencolumbcille in Donegal, Maam Valley, the lakes in Connemara, or ribbons of road out the Dingle peninsula, the Burren is one of those places that quieten and make you giddy at the same time. It is full of mystery and surprise, stones and flowers. Nothing had happened there, it seemed, for all eternity. And in that, for me, lay so much of its attraction. The spiritual sense of the Irish landscape has always been as real as the rain to Chris and to me. There's a kind of untouched, untouchable holiness in places that seeps inside you.

On the day I was to collect Chris in Lisdoonvarna, feeling still radiant with new fatherhood, I wanted to slip from the world and climb for an hour in the peace of the Burren. Pamela came up to baby-sit. Martin Murray came with Tim Robinson's marvelous walking map of the area, and said he would join me. We took the Peugeot to the coast road and drove to the heart of that sound.

Boireann means a rocky place, and among the millions

of its rocks are over 450 ring forts and 66 megalithic tombs of limestone slabs. The Burren is a home for wild orchids, blue gentians, violets, potentilia, bluebells, and a whole cluster of other rare plants more suited to the Mediterranean than the coast of north Clare. For its southern boundaries the map showed Kilnaboy, Kilfenora, Lisdoonvarna, and Doolin, to the north, Black Head, Ballyvaughan, and the Flaggy Shore at New Quay. Where in all this fissured and flowered expanse of rock was Chris with her palette, brushes, and canvas that morning? Although the deep and remarkable Aillwee Cave at the center of the Burren is one of its most popular attractions, that morning I wanted to climb above the sea to one of the limestone plateaus that look down into the blue waters of Galway Bay.

"What about . . . Gleninagh Mountain, one thousand and forty-five feet," said Martin, poring over the map in the passenger seat. "*Dobhach Brainin*, it says, is at the top of it."

"Where is it?" I asked, leaning over to look.

"Right there," he said pointing to where a gray sweep of rock rose out of sight above us.

"Gleninagh Mountain it is," I said, and pulled the Peugeot to the side of the road.

Half an hour later we were, if not exactly climbing, pushing our way upwards through the scrub to the first shelving of the rock. As I moved with elbows raised through goat gaps in the brown briers and bracken, I could see bright specks of tiny flowers in the stones above. Then, it was all stone. We reached a first plateau and suddenly great cracked pavements, for all the world like the walkways of ancient gods, stretched in front of us and then rose into the rock face. They were fissured in a million places, some openings a man's hand could just squeeze into, others had a sharp-edged stone deliberately jagged into them. Who had put them there, and why? Climbers?

Herdsmen? They stuck up eerily like so many signs, and I passed them with a little shiver of apprehension. The whole surface of the mountain seemed strange to me. Because the limestone was porous, the rocks were full of scoops and hollows worked into it by centuries of rainfall, and now pocking it with weird water prints like the steps of giants. In many of them, minute flowers shot up, blooming in the frostless crags where few people ever saw them.

Sweat was pouring off me now. Martin was a few yards above my head and going strong. He waited for me at a high stone wall, built onto the rock slope of the mountain itself and dividing nothing but stone from stone. We sat down for a breather. The sea was already far below, the air sweet and fresh and cool. How easy it was just to sit there, gazing away at the three humped whales of the Aran Islands in the blue bay, and imagining how infinitely tiny, two dabs of color, we must seem from the road. I took out the map. My hands were a little chalky from the climb and felt smooth upon the paper. My eye fell on notations in the map where others had left marks in the stone; in small print I read: Blessed Bush and Marks of St. Brigid's Knees; Hoofprints of Glas Ghaibhneach Cow; Holy Well (Toothache Cure); Mark of Saint's Fingers in Stone; *Tobar Cholmain*, Arched Stone for Headache Cure; *Cnoc Fionn*, Site for MacClancy Law School, 16th Century; Caves of the Wild Horses, and perhaps most curious of all, something called a Strange Field in the area known as Cragballyconoal. These names conjured up amazing scenes. I put away the map and we climbed on.

Away to the left of us, our only companions, a small herd of goats, moved sure footedly along the mountain. The rock face was becoming steeper now and we went without a word, hurrying upwards, drawn towards the top. Another crest, another plateau, and again another crest beyond it. It rose in shelves, each one a little cooler, cleaner, *emptier* than the last

Neither of us were mountain climbers of any description; in America, I thought, this would be a hill not a mountain, and yet the feeling as we came to the mounded ring of stones that was *Dobhach Brainin* was a mountain climber's feeling. A feeling of having arrived. In a hush, we sat down. For miles and miles nothing but gray stone swept away into the distance on all sides of us. There was no sound, but for a little breeze that whispered now and then across the cairn top. It was the quietest place I had ever been in my life. Martin opened a flask of strong tea. I felt there was something missing, something not quite right. And then, high above us a first bird darted across the sky and down onto the stones. Then another. Then two more, three more, and suddenly the air was all birdsong about us. We were sitting there now quiet as the stones while clusters of birds came and went in songful delight. After a time I looked up and saw a hawk arcing overhead us in the silence, in his unmoving eye a moving panorama of all the west, the mountainous brown, gray and green splendor of it. Another bird, wind-balancing in midflight, sang out madly to the sight of sunshine in Galway, and I sat there watching him.

Hours later, I drove to Lisdoonvarna to collect Chris. She had spent the day not far from me, painting on the other side of the same mountain. Back in Kiltumper that evening, she would tell me she was unhappy with her Burren painting even as I am unhappy with anything I have been able to write about the Burren. It's a part of the mysterious attraction of the Burren to me; it escapes the constrictions of definition, yet dwells on in memory, like that lone songbird swooping and climbing through the air, cawing, screaming, and singing between the stones and the sea with nobody to hear for miles around.

A bit overcast today after two weeks of pure sunshine. There's a gray cover blocking the spring sun but it's a perfect day for planting the plants I got yesterday. Violas — purple and yellow—Canterbury bells, thyme, purple arabis, rock garden poppies, flax, and blue-eyed grass like the kind that used to grow at the bottom of our driveway where I waited for the school bus back home in Katonah, New York. What a sweet surprise to find it here.

It's a day for moving things around, too. A lupin over there and the peonies in the open space beside the pink spirea. The oriental poppies have tripled in size and look vibrant and healthy but too abundant. One has to go. It'll get smothered by the yellow lupin otherwise. The perennial cornflower needs a better spot and the dwarf asters, already damaged by those blasted slugs, are lost where they are and need to be moved to the front of the border.

I worked two hours in the morning while Deirdre took her nap and two hours again in the afternoon. By evening I was "knackered," as they say in Dublin after a hard day's work. Over supper I told Niall of all the work I had done and that it had been a perfect day for planting. And, I added, "I hope it rains tomorrow, the garden really needs it." He laughed and said, "Is there no pleasing you?"

April 16, Deirdre's first birthday. About two weeks ago we decided to have a double celebration: a birthday party along with the special ceremony for the christening of adopted children. Down in the village I asked Father Leenane to perform the ceremony. Yes, he said, of course he would, and then, added: What about having the christening up at the house? We were delighted. It seemed to Chris and me especially fitting that Deirdre should be christened here in the kitchen of the old house in Kiltumper. Chris sent out the invitation cards. She held one up for Deirdre to look at and, to help prepare her, sang little whispery snippets of "Happy Birthday" into the baby's amazed ears. In the same week Deirdre took her first really *confident* long walk across the kitchen and back, giggling to herself as she crossed from the cupboard to my knee, clapping her hands when we applauded her and moving with a funny kind of quick slap-down steps that kept her miraculously balanced as she went back and forth. Almost one year old and coming at the world with lovely laughing blue eyes and tottering quick steps, giddy with joy.

The party was all set. All of our neighbors were invited. We ordered a special strawberry mousse birthday cake in Ennis. Our neighbors added a feast of home baking: fresh brown and white scones, Queen cakes, apple and rhubarb tarts, sponge cakes of all kinds, with cream and without, with slices of oranges, mandarins, or strawberries. I collected a second table and two folding chairs from Mary that morning. Two more arrived from Dooleys'. Three long benches (or forms as they are called in this part of the country) were brought up from the village hall and set across the kitchen. Tessie sent up her large teapot, and from Lucy came two dozen glasses; china cups, saucers, and plates; spoons, knives, and forks.

With that we were ready. By mid morning Pamela and

Mary Murray had arrived to help. There were over thirty people invited, and we wondered a little at how we would fit them all around the priest for the ceremony. There was no time to worry about it. Deirdre was tottering around the kitchen and looking at everything. What were these benches doing across the space she walked in? What were all these brightly colored balloons that hung from the beams of the kitchen ceiling? What were all these cards and cakes and that song she kept hearing—"Happy Birthday to You"? I saw the world through her one-year-old eyes that morning. She knew that something special was happening, and happening for her at that. When she was party-dressed in her pink dress with stitchwork smocking that Chris's mother had sent her, and her long white stockings and little white shoes, I thought I saw in her a newer radiance still, a happiness that rubbed off on everyone who saw her.

By three o'clock that day, April 16, our kitchen was abuzz with friends and neighbors. All the food had been moved into the parlor and at the round kitchen table, Father Leenane set the christening candle to begin the ceremony. A hush fell. Lucy and Larry, as godparents, sat up next to us and we heard Father Leenane's gentle voice say the opening prayers. "We have come together today to share the joy of Crissie and Niall as they thank God for the gift of this child."

The gift of this child. My heart was standing still, I couldn't breathe. The gift of this child. In a kind of half dream the prayers washed over us. When we reached the Prayer of Parents and Chris and I started to read, "With joy we welcome Deirdre into our home, with joy we take her to our hearts," there were tears in Chris's voice. The words slipped from us in a half whisper and Chris reached to steady the shake of my hand as it held out the prayer sheet.

"May God, who has begun this good work, bring it to perfection," said Father Leenane, and then, from Jay and Tessie's lovely young daughter Mareid, came the first of the Prayers of the Participants.

"Lord Jesus, may Deirdre find love, happiness, and care in her new home. May she grow up to love the Lord God with all her heart, and her neighbor as herself. Lord, hear our prayer."

The words struck me with the force of a blow. There, all around us, were our neighbors and friends. What welcome and generosity they had extended to us since the very first day we had arrived here among them. They were truly warm hearted, I thought, and a wave of gratitude came over me for all the unasked-for little things these people had done for us. How they had watched out for us, helped us with everything from cows and calves to chimneys and chairs, and for so long, with cups of tea and fireside talk, shared in our hope to adopt this baby girl.

And love her neighbor as herself. It rang so true for me there in the kitchen that afternoon, like the key to the whole notion of people living together. And if we had managed to move our lives successfully from America to a quiet townland in west Clare, then these good people were the reason, and for all they had and continued to do for us I could never thank them enough.

We were reaching the end of the ceremony. "Together, we are all adopted children of our common Father," said Father Leenane, coming to the final blessing. "Almighty God, giver of life, look with favor on Crissie and Niall. May they be blessed in their child and ever grow closer in their love for each other. May Almighty God bless you . . . and you, little Deirdre," he said bending down to her, "in the name of the Father, and the Son, and the Holy Spirit, Amen."

Everyone came forward with handshakes and congratulations. And even as somebody was putting on the kettle and getting ready with the first round of cakes, Chris turned to kiss me, and we both looked down to where, below my knee, one-year-old Deirdre was clinging to a green balloon and smiling up at the world of faces smiling down at her.

Evelyn and Una Downes came this afternoon each carrying a fistful of flowers which they had collected on the way: yellow cowslips, violets, ferns, a twig of the blackthorn's white blossoms, and some creeping speedwell. All around, the blackthorn is in bloom, drifts of tiny white flowers on leafless, crooked branches. And the gorse, yellow fruity blossoms of springtime, liven the hillsides like buttercups.

Dad arrived today for one of his quick, flying visits and we got him outside into the garden. He was delighted to be out with us in the misty rain. All three of us were in our rain gear digging the earth and weeding. We planted the remainder of the onion sets and another furrow of carrots and prepared further beds for the cauliflowers, debating whether that leftover patch should be a triangular bed or not. Afterwards, Wellies and rain gear put away, we dressed in our best and were treated, in honor of my birthday, to a superb dinner at the famous Dromoland

Castle, on whose grounds stand three-hundred-year-old trees like nature's giant sculptures and where the food is exquisite *and* expensive.

How is it all going, then? Nine-week-old chicks chirped in a cardboard box in the corner as Ann and Noel Butler sat down on the couch in the kitchen and looked around them. Having read the chronicle of our first year's adventures here, they had written to us from New Jersey and asked if they might stop by on their next visit to Ireland. We had had other visitors already, but these were the first to write to us of their intent. When we first realized that people might want to stop by and see us, we had been a little cautious, for it seemed to Chris and me that no matter how scrupulously we had adhered to the truth in writing of Kiltumper, the moment something was written down it seemed to take on a life of its own. Kiltumper is not an idyll; it is an out-of-the-way place in the wilds of Clare. It has all the drawbacks of the west of Ireland today, as well as all the beauty. Our home is neither exotic nor impressive, and there were a hundred things through the house and garden that needed doing. And yet, for us this has become the place invested with our dream of a simpler life, and now, as letters from America arrive in our biscuit-tin letter box, we feel a little like ambassadors of that dream.

How is it all going? every letter asks. Were we still here? Were the cows all right? How was Mary? How was the turf this year? How are the ducks, Larry, Darrell, and Darrell? Is the Peugeot still running? Did we get pigs?

As the spring drew on, the bundle of letters we keep in a wicker basket grew ever larger. There were messages from places like Prairie Village, Kansas; Sparta, Tennessee; Manitoba, Canada; Northfield, Minnesota; Malden, Massachusetts; Waco, Texas; Little Rock, Arkansas; Warren, Vermont; South Bend, Indiana; Omaha, Nebraska; Des Plaines, Illinois; Sparks, Maryland; Lexington, Kentucky; Parma, Ohio; Pottstown, Pennsylvania; and dozens of other towns and cities across America where a common feeling for Ireland lives on. To each and all of them these pages are meant as our reply.

Yes, it is all going fine. This year the first days of summer saw the garden blossom as never before. Down the path the lupins shot up like crazy, great yellow and purple spires of them loomed five feet tall and dwarfed almost everything. There were red and pink poppies everywhere, clusters of daisies and columbines and delphiniums, roses and lilies and liatrus, and dahlias and asters and annuals. In the fine weather of April, I had been able to set the potatoes earlier than before, wheeling barrows of dung into the western side of the garden and forking it into the furrows with a now familiar feeling of trust and hope. The rhythms of this place are our rhythms now. By June, standing on the path with his brother Karol and giving us the wisdom of his eleven years, Francie told me we had fine stalks. Ridges of onions, lazy beds full of cauliflowers and brussel sprouts, a tangle of dwarf variety sugar snap peas on the pea fence and Chris's three deep-dug beds of carrots were all growing once more. And to them all Deirdre gave an inspector's approval, toddling out the kitchen door and through the flowers at every opportunity and bending down and stroking brightly colored blossoms like so many pets. "Nice flowers, yes, Deirdre, nice flowers."

On the farm, the spring cycle has begun again. The

cows all calved, this year without assistance, and their calves run and kick in the new grass in Lower Tumper, sometimes chased by the black goat with the blue rope headdress. On summer mornings I like to walk out early across the dew-wet fields, watching a few white-tailed hares scurry off over the grass and the birds scattering into the morning sky. In the absolute hush of Irish fields in the empty morning, I have the sense that nothing matters anywhere but this, the plumed turf smoke from the cottage chimney and the loveliness of Ireland on a summer morning. No matter how long we live here, I think we will never lose this. For this quality of life in the west of Ireland, the timelessness of its beauty, the sense all around you of weather and land, has brought to both Chris and me an extraordinary peace.

Sometimes in the mornings Chris comes with me, and we carry the baby on our shoulders. Coming up to our little herd, Deirdre cries "Moo, Moo" and points to cows and calves alike. The old cows seem at first to turn a specially quizzical eye upon the child, as if taking in our new circumstances, and then low contentedly. In the tiniest pair of blue Wellies, Deirdre totters forward among the animals, and smiles when the cows move aside for her.

Once again it is summer. As I write, it is a glorious day in June. For twenty-one days the sun has shone down relentlessly upon us. The meadows are full of early hay, and there are trams of it everywhere. The evenings gleam brightly until nearly midnight and the light seems never quite to die. Now every window in the house is open to take in the day. Earlier this morning Chris was outside at her easel in a wide-brimmed sunhat working on a large canvas of the front of the house and the summer garden. By noon, she came in and told me, laughing, that it was almost too hot to paint.

More readers of our first book walked up the garden

path yesterday, bringing jars of peanut butter and Jiffy corn bread mix. At lunchtime we sat outside with sandwiches. The sun flooded the garden with light. Nobody came or went on the road outside, birds flickered between the flowers in a summer dance. There was hardly a sound anywhere. Away across from us on Hayes' Hill, four brown horses galloped in the sunshine. In her journal Chris made a note: "Another sparkling blue day. Not a cloud anywhere. No haze or whiteness in the sky, just deep, deep blue that goes on forever. Today Ireland seems like an island in the sun. It's hot and still and blue and green everywhere. Just remarkable."

Now, this afternoon, as I write these words, my head full of thoughts of endings and beginnings, of the time we have been here and the long days of summers yet ahead of us, I hear Chris in the kitchen telling Deirdre a story she intends to write for her, a story that might have been told to children on these hills long centuries ago. Now, like a continuing cycle worked into the land and air like springs and summers themselves, I hear Chris's voice begin "Once upon a time, there was a giant called Tumper . . ."

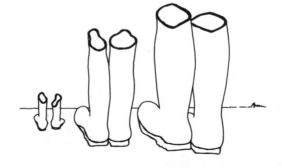

ABOUT THE AUTHORS

Niall Williams was born and raised in Dublin. He has an M.A. in American Literature from University College Dublin and a Certificate in Farming from the Irish Agricultural Advisory Board.

Christine Breen was born in New Jersey and grew up in suburban Westchester County, New York. She is a graduate of Boston College and was studying Irish Literature at U.C.D. when she met Niall. They were wed in 1981.

They worked in publishing in New York before deciding to become small farmers. They live now in the cottage in which Christine's grandfather was born near the village of Kilmihil in County Clare.

Together they have written *O Come Ye Back to Ireland* and *When Summer's In the Meadow* telling of their new lives.